THE WRITING of Indian mission history has long focused on initial periods of contact when missionaries played crucial roles in culture encounter. Only rarely does any study go beyond those first years to give us a glimpse of native people, both Christians and traditionalists, struggling to survive in a strange and hostile world. . . . Examining the lives of eighteenth-century Christian Indians suggests important lessons about both mission history and the wider field of native experience. The diary and letters of Joseph Fish provide just that sort of window into native life in the eighteenth century. . . . The text is cleanly presented without destroying its flavor and authentic character. The annotations are both useful and restrained. More important, in valuable comments before and after the documents proper, the editors provide thoughtful analysis of both Narragansett Christians and their often bewildered missionary. This is a superb book and one that deserves a wide and appreciative audience.

—James P. Ronda, *Rhode Island History*

WILLIAM S. SIMMONS, Professor of Anthropology at the University of California, Berkeley, is author of *Cautantowwit's House* (1970) and *Eyes of the Night: Witchcraft Among a Senegalese People* (1971), coauthor of *Man Makes Sense: A Reader in Modern Cultural Anthropology* (1970), and has written numerous articles in scholarly and semipopular periodicals. CHERYL L. SIMMONS has worked for several years as a Research Assistant in the Anthropology Department at Berkeley.

Cover illustration taken from 1839 engraving of Eleazar Wheelock and Indian students by Samuel E. Brown.

Old Light
on Separate Ways

The Narragansett Diary of
Joseph Fish
1765-1776

William S. Simmons

AND

Cheryl L. Simmons

EDITORS

University Press of New England
HANOVER AND LONDON, 1982

Publication of this volume has been aided by a grant from the NATIONAL ENDOWMENT FOR THE HUMANITIES.

Copyright © 1982 Trustees of Dartmouth College

Library of Congress Cataloging in Publication Data

Fish, Joseph, 1706-1781.
  Old light on separate ways.

  Includes bibliographical references and index.
  1. Narraganset Indians—Missions. 2. Indians of North America—Rhode Island—Missions. 3. Congregationalist churches—Missions—Rhode Island. 4. Fish, Joseph, 1706-1781. I. Simmons, William Scranton, 1938-   II. Simmons, Cheryl L. III. Title.
E99.N16F57   1982   266'.587459   81-71906
ISBN 0-87451-239-5   AACR2

To Our Parents

CONTENTS

An illustration insert follows page 121

PREFACE

THE MANUSCRIPTS

The Narragansett Diary of Joseph Fish is a series of seven manuscript notebooks that he kept for the commissioners, in Boston, of the Company for Propagation of the Gospel in New England and the parts adjacent in America (also known as the New England Company) to account for his journeys and expenses while in their service as a missionary to the Narragansett Indian community in Charlestown, Rhode Island. These notebooks are in the Manuscript Collections of the Connecticut Historical Society, to which they were donated in the nineteenth century by the Reverend John Noyes who was a grandson of Joseph Fish.[1] The bindings are stitched by hand, and the pages measure approximately 3⅞ by 6¼ inches. They are in good condition, and for the most part Fish's writing is fairly legible. Each book is numbered, and although originally there were ten, three are missing:

1. November 26, 1765 — September 3, 1766 (15 pages)
2. October 1, 1766 — October 14, 1767 (14 pages)
3. Missing
4. June 20, 1768 — November 7, 1768 (22 pages)

[1] Noyes, the son of Fish's elder daughter, Mary, died May 15, 1846, in his eighty-fourth year (Morris 1857: 362). Fish kept brief diary notebooks of his missionary activities among the Pequot Indians of Stonington, Connecticut, which Noyes also donated to the Connecticut Historical Society. Because Pequot history is separate and distinct from that of the Narragansett, these diaries are not included in this volume. Neither the Narragansett nor the Pequot diaries of the Reverend Joseph Fish have been previously published, nor are they mentioned in Forbes's *New England Diaries 1602-1800*... or in Matthews's *American Diaries in Manuscript, 1580-1954: A Descriptive Bibliography*.

5. January 2, 1769 — October 23, 1769   (19 pages)
6. Missing
7. September 24, 1770 — May 6, 1771   (28 pages)
8. May 27, 1771 — May 11, 1772   (38 pages)
9. Missing
10. May 10, 1773 — January 22, 1776   (51 pages)

Fish's correspondence regarding his Narragansett missionary work supplement the diary; thirteen of these (eleven from the Manuscript Collections of the Connecticut Historical Society and two from the Manuscript Collections of the Dartmouth College Library) have been inserted in the text.

THE EDITORIAL METHOD

In transcribing the Narragansett Diary and correspondence we intended to make the text intelligible to the modern reader while preserving as much of its original form and flavor as possible. We consulted the editorial guidelines established by Boyd et al. (1950: vii-xxxviii), Butterfield et al. (1961: lv-lix), Handlin et al. (1954: 94-104), Jordan (1962: xi), and McLoughlin (1979, I: xxxiii-xxxvii), choosing from these the rules that applied best to the Fish manuscripts and improvising to some extent to accommodate the idiosyncrasies of this particular material.

Spelling. Although Fish's spelling is often inconsistent, we have retained the original spelling and have not burdened the text with sics to call attention to his errors. Obvious slips of the pen have been corrected without comment.

Capitalization. We preserved the form of the original with the exception that all sentences start with capital letters regardless of the way they appear in the manuscript. Fish capitalized liberally, and often there was very little differentiation between his capital and small case letters, making accurate transcription difficult. We followed his usage as closely as possible, and if there was any serious question as to whether a given letter was capital or not, we followed modern usage.

Punctuation. Original punctuation has been retained with the following four exceptions: (1) every sentence ends with a period, (2) dashes intended to be terminal marks are converted to periods, (3) superfluous dashes (that is, those which occur after periods) are eliminated, (4) if a passage is misleading or unclear because of missing or incorrect punctuation, minimal punctuation for intelligibility is supplied. If, however, the passage could have more than one meaning, the punctuation is left exactly as it stands in the original.

Abbreviations and Contractions. These have been normally expanded and the superscript letters have been lowered to the line of the text and a period supplied. The ampersand, the thorn, and the symbol (denoting per, pre, or pro) are among the forms that have been consistently expanded. The tilde, when it occurs, has been deleted, and the letter it represents has been added in its place. The following, however, will be retained in their original form: (1) names of persons, (2) names of geographical places, (3) dates, (4) books of the Bible, (5) monetary designations, (6) units of weight and measurement, (7) the dateline, salutation, and complimentary close of letters,[2] and (8)

---

[2] In the several cases where the thorn appears in the dateline of letters we expanded the thorn to "the." In other respects datelines

those abbreviations still in use today and thus easily recognizable to the modern reader, such as Mr., Esqr., and Revd. In the rare case where an abbreviation or contraction in the original is unclear owing to a misspelling or an irregular form and, in accordance with the rules stated above, it is to remain literal, the letter (s) necessary for intelligibility have been supplied within square brackets.

Interlineations. These are brought down to the line of the text where the author intended them to be. Oddly spaced material, such as that written in the margins or crosswise on the page, is noted by the use of square brackets with the location of the material noted within: [Inserted inverted in the left margin: Copy sent to Doctr. Babcock]. With regard to letters, no matter where the address appears on the original, we have routinely placed it at the head of the letter, situated above the date and salutation.

Cancelled Passages. All have been disregarded.

Missing or Illegible Matter. When a word or part thereof is missing, but it is clear from the context what it is, the missing element will be added within square brackets: [Sachem] or [mi]nistry. When a reading is conjectural a question mark will precede it within square brackets: [?Labours]. When material is completely illegible, this is noted by three suspension points within square brackets, [. . .], or by four suspension points if the material comes at the end of a sentence, [. . . .].

Editor's Omissions. These are noted by three suspension points if the omission entails only part of a sentence, and

---

are kept literal, though placement on the page has been standardized herein.

four suspension points if it comes at the end of a sentence or if it entails more than a sentence but less than a paragraph. An entire row of suspension points is used if the omission includes a paragraph or more.

The following material, all specific to the Fish texts, was uniformly deleted without suspension points: (1) all pagination on the original diary notebooks and letters; (2) repetitious headings at the top of the pages of the diary notebooks, i.e., "Journeys to Narraganset," "Journeys etc."; (3) words in the bottom right-hand corner of the page that the author used as pagination guides, i.e., *"verte,"* or more commonly, the first word of the following page; and (4) relisted table headings, i.e., when the author carried over a table to the following page, he frequently relisted the heading on that page. These have been omitted. We uniformly deleted (with suspension points) the words "First Journey," "Second Journey," etc., which routinely appear in the original either immediately preceding or following the date at the start of each entry in the diary notebooks.

The pages of the diary are short and its structure so repetitive that the material mentioned above was eliminated to enhance readability. Also, we deleted most of his accounting regarding the salary and expenses he applied for and received from the New England Company, repetitious material, and some details regarding travel, the weather, and where he lodged. The wording of the titles of some books was slightly rearranged for purposes of consistency.

Acknowledgments

We are grateful to Thompson R. Harlow, director of the Connecticut Historical Society, for permission to edit and publish the Fish diary and correspondence, and to Kenneth C. Cramer, archivist of the Dartmouth College Library, for permission to publish transcriptions of two letters from the Eleazar Wheelock Papers. We also wish to thank Richard Champlin of the Redwood Library for his generous help in tracking down numerous details regarding persons named in the texts. For the support given us and this project over the last several years by the University of California, Berkeley, and by the staff of the Berkeley Anthropology Department, we are especially grateful.

Many other individuals kindly helped answer questions and locate materials that contributed to the completion of this work. These include Harold Kemble and Glenn LaFantasie of the Rhode Island Historical Society; Mark Keller, who located and provided copies of Indian-related material from the Champlin Papers in the Rhode Island Historical Society; Ruth Blair, of the Connecticut Historical Society, who helped with questions and requests regarding the Fish manuscripts; Phyllis Silva, of the Rhode Island State Archives, who furnished us with copies of several manuscript documents pertaining to the Narragansett tribe; and Patricia Wolfston, who located and transcribed materials from the manuscript collections of the Guildhall Library, London. We also thank Mary Plummer, of the Presbyterian Historical Society, Harold Worthley, of the Congregational Library, and C. R. Cooper, of the Guildhall Library, for answering questions regarding their archival holdings. James Axtell, James Ronda (see Ronda and Axtell 1978), Neal Salisbury (see Salisbury 1982), Ives Goddard, and William Sturtevant have been valuable sources of information regarding early American ethnohistorical materials, and Eric Thomas has been a helpful guide to many aspects of Narragansett history. Francis Jennings, Neal Salisbury, and Eric Thomas read the manuscript and kindly offered a number of insightful criticisms.

In addition to the individuals whose contributions have been indicated, we wish to acknowledge the friendly co-operation of the staffs of the American Antiquarian Society, the Connecticut Historical Society Library, Dartmouth College Library, the John Carter Brown Library, the Yale University Library, the Massachusetts Historical Society Library, the Huntington Library, the Redwood Library, the Rockefeller Library, the Newport Historical Society Library, the United Society for the Propagation of the Gospel, London, the Westerly and Charlestown, Rhode Island, town halls, and the Interlibrary Loan Department of the Doe Library at Berkeley. Finally, we wish to extend our appreciation to Grace Buzaljko for her editorial insights and to Carol Dows for her careful typing.

William Simmons assembled the Fish documents from their several locations and did all research regarding interpretive, illustrative, and footnote material, in addition to determining which parts of the manuscript were to be deleted or retained. Cheryl Simmons did all transcriptions and all research related to editorial method.

Joseph Fish
and the Narragansett

JOSEPH FISH
AND THE NARRAGANSETT

Anthropologists and historians have written extensively about New England Indians and Indian-White relations in the seventeenth century but have only begun to interpret the subsequent three centuries of adjustment by these Indians to Euro-American society. Although most violent conflict between Indian and English societies ceased in this region after King Philip's War in 1676, economic and political conflict continued to characterize relations between the Indian remnants and the colonial society upon which they depended. Throughout the post-contact period Indians lived a vulnerable existence around the periphery of American society, where they were both protected and discriminated against by local governments and where they struggled to hold on to the land and other resources they still possessed.[1]

The Narragansett Diary of Reverend Joseph Fish is important because it offers an eyewitness account of Narragansett Indian life in the mid eighteenth century, a time when the Narragansett had internalized many aspects of English culture and were desperately striving to preserve what remained of their dwindling reservation. Fish arrived among the Narragansett in the midst of an intense legal and political conflict between the royal head of the tribe,

[1] Several important studies of post-seventeenth-century Indian life in New England have been done recently by Boissevain (1975), Bragdon (1979: 136-41; 1981), Brasser (1974), Campbell and LaFantasie (1978: 67-83), Conkey, Boissevain, and Goddard (1978: 177-89), Day (1981), Hutchins (1979), Levitas (1980), Ronda (1981: 369-94), and Simmons (1982). For an overall account or eighteenth-century Indian missions in New England see Bowden (1981: 134-44).

Sachem Thomas Ninigret, and a populist religious leader, the Christian Indian minister Samuel Niles, who was trying to prevent the Sachem from selling reservation property to the English. The diary and other correspondence reveal an interesting intercultural dialogue between Fish, a Harvard-educated Puritan, and the faction of the Narragansett community that adhered to Niles and belonged to the Narragansett Church. Many Narragansett had converted to Christianity during the enthusiasm of the Great Awakening of the 1740s and strongly identified with the beliefs and practices of the Separate and Separate Baptist churches, whose doctrines Fish abhorred. In recording his disapproval of their beliefs as well as their criticisms of his, Fish gives insight into Narragansett world view at this period of their transformation into an Indian Yankee people.

JOSEPH FISH

Joseph Fish was born of a Pilgrim lineage in Duxbury, Massachusetts, on January 28, 1705. After completing study for the ministry at Harvard College, he accepted an invitation from the Second Church of North Stonington, Connecticut to be their pastor and served there from 1732 until his death on May 26, 1781.[2] In appearance,

[2] The principal biographical accounts of Joseph Fish are those by Hubbell (1863), Morris (1857: 359-63), Shipton (1951, VIII: 417-26), and Silliman (1857: 363-66). Details of his life are mentioned in numerous other sources including Allen (1857: 352), Haynes (1949: 34), Norton (1976: 515-29), Trumbull (1818, II: 171-72), and Wheeler (1900: 374). Fish kept a diary of his most intimate spiritual feelings, mainly during the Great Awakening, which is now among the Silliman Family Papers (Ms. 450) in the Yale University Library. Numerous manuscript letters by Fish are in the possession of the American Antiquarian Society, the Connecticut Historical Society, the Massachusetts Historical Society, Dartmouth College Library, and the Yale University Library.

according to one of his parishioners, "he was tall and very well proportioned; his complexion rather light; his eyes expressive and benignant; his gait dignified and graceful; and his whole bearing impressive and agreeable" (**Hubbell** 1863: 9-10). In 1732 he married Rebecca Pabodie of Little Compton, Rhode Island, who was a great-granddaughter of John Alden of the *Mayflower*, and together they had two daughters, Mary and Rebecca. Their **grandson,** Professor Benjamin Silliman of Yale College, wrote of them that "the religious sentiments, the social character, and domestic manners, of the Puritans [were] . . . transmitted to Mr. and Mrs. Fish, in whom they appeared distinct and pure, but softened and refined" (**Silliman** 1857: 363). In raising their children they emphasized the values of prayer, study, and work: "Their studies and books, their domestic training in the duties of house keeping . . . and the rites of hospitality and of personal and family religion, filled their time, so that they were rarely without employment, and even casual idleness sometimes received a mild, paternal rebuke" (Ibid. 364).

To Joseph Fish, as to many English Puritans, "theology was wedded to politics and politics to the progress of the kingdom of God" (Bercovitch 1978: xiv). For example, when General James Wolfe captured Quebec from the French in 1759, Fish told his audience: "The Lord has brought us, thro' a Field of Blood, into the strong City Quebec, the capital of our Enemies Country; to set up his own Worship there, where Saints and Images had been long adored" (Fish 1760: 36). He strongly supported the American cause in the Revolution and in 1776 urged young Connecticut men to join General Washington against the British:

We that are old cannot go forth to the war. Were it not that my nerves are unstrung and my limbs enfeebled with age, in such a cause as you have, I think I should willingly quit the pulpit, put off my priestly garments, buckle on the harness, and with trumpet in hand, hasten to the battle. (Hubbell 1863: 15)

Fish was as attentive to the religious meaning of his own moods and feelings as he was to the significance of war, politics, and other external events, and often doubted his adequacy for the ministry. For Fish and many other Puritans, self-doubt and self-examination regarding his own worthiness for salvation proved to be an incentive for renewed efforts in his spiritual life, his family relationships, and his pastoral work.

His fifty-year ministry covered an eventful period in American social history. Growth in population combined with an increase in commerce and a shortage of land helped create sharpening distinctions between rich and poor and new patterns of social as well as geographical mobility. As individuals pushed against traditional values and institutions to achieve greater economic and political ambitions, or simply to survive, many also questioned the churches that helped bind the traditional order together— imperceptibly at first through decline in religious zeal and then massively in the Great Awakening of 1740–45.[3] The English evangelist George Whitefield, who was the master spokesman for the revival, arrived in New England in the fall of 1740 to a series of enthusiastic receptions. Whitefield appealed because of his remarkable gift for preaching but also, according to Gary B. Nash, because he "frontally

[3] For more extensive discussions of early to mid eighteenth-century social history in this area see Bushman (1967), Daniels (1980: 429-50), Lockridge (1973: 403-39), McLoughlin (1978: 45-80), and Nash (1979: 198-219). The principal accounts of the Great Awakening in New England are those by Gaustad (1957), Goen (1962), and Tracy (1842).

challenged traditional sources of authority, called upon people to become the instruments of their own salvation, and implicitly attacked the prevailing upper-class notion that the uneducated mass of people had no minds of their own" (Nash 1979: 206). In an analysis of the interaction of social and religious change in eighteenth-century Connecticut, Richard L. Bushman concluded that the Great Awakening provided a breakthrough for those with reasons to challenge communal restraints: "Far from instilling submission to the old authority, the revival planted the conviction that God's power was given to individuals, clearing the way for men to resist in good conscience when the occasion arose" (Bushman 1967: 267).

The Great Awakening permanently affected Fish's personal and professional life. In company with many Standing, or established, ministers he first welcomed the revival that followed George Whitefield's visit to New England in 1740, both for the swelling of personal religious enthusiasm and for the surge in church attendance caused by the revival. Looking back upon this early period of the Awakening some years later, Fish wrote:

... about twenty three and twenty four years ago, there was the most wonderful work of God, that was ever known, in this part of the world. ... It seems there was a general thoughtfulness about religion prevailing in the minds of people. ... The ministers of Christ were stirred up to preach, with uncommon zeal and solemnity, and the people as ready to hear, with unusual attention, while the things of eternity were charged hence to the conscience. ... the ears of the people were thus opened to hear, and their hearts awake to receive instruction. (Fish 1767: 114)

Whitefield had introduced a dramatic and emotional style of religious oratory that appealed to thousands of Americans who had never seen the like. He was quickly imitated by numerous ministers and laymen who became known as itinerants because of their practice of traveling from one community to another to preach. The most flamboyant of the itinerants, the Reverend James Davenport, of Southold, Long Island, preached in the Stonington area in summer, 1741, and "one hundred are said to have been awakened under his first sermon" (Sprague 1858, III: 82). Davenport and other radical itinerants assaulted the core of Puritan culture with which Fish identified. First, they introduced religious experiences such as revelations, visions, trances, and emotional participation in services, which were offensive to the more orderly and intellectual Puritanism of the seventeenth and early eighteenth centuries. They also challenged the legitimacy of the Standing clergy on the grounds that their written and learned sermons came from the mind and not the heart and lacked the power to affect the unconverted. Davenport, Isaac Backus, and others taught that ministers like Reverend Fish, who owed their authority only to learning and not to immediate revelation, were unconverted and incapable of saving others. They further condemned clergymen who drew public salaries as hirelings who preached for love of money rather than for love of God.[4] As a result of the itinerants' charges and the resistance which their teaching inevitably stirred up among the Standing clergy, large numbers of New Light converts defected from established churches to follow Separate preachers who attributed their

---

4 The Standing ministers in Massachusetts and Connecticut at this time were supported by mandatory public taxation. Although Anglicans, Quakers, and Baptists had been exempt from religious taxes since 1727, New Light dissenters (Separates), were not exempt and resented the obligation to contribute to the support of the established clergy whose legitimacy they challenged. In Rhode Island, where no state church had ever existed, clergymen of all denominations were supported by voluntary contributions from their parishioners.

mandate to spontaneous experience—what Backus referred to as the "internal call," as opposed to the "external call" conferred through college study (Backus 1754). As the Separate movement spread, many people, including the poor, common, and uneducated saw it as an opportunity to rebel against the Standing religious order. Davenport was particularly disruptive because he "indicted the rich and powerful, criticized the yawning gap between the rich and poor, and exhorted ordinary people to resist those who exploited and deceived them" (Nash 1979: 210). According to Fish, who lost two-thirds of his North Stonington congregation to the Separates and Separate Baptists, the radical New Lights "would hear *none* of them preach but such as they esteemed LIVELY preachers: and accordingly would leave the *house* and *worship* of God, if the spirit happened to be *one* whom they did not esteem to be *converted, lively, powerful,* etc." (Fish 1767: 141).[5] Backus replied that Fish's own sermons were "a proper specimen of that treatment which *scattered* Christ's sheep in that day" (McLoughlin 1968: 249).

In their emphasis on spontaneity, revelations, the internal call, and strict separation of the pure from the unconverted, the Separates and Separate Baptists rediscovered basic symbols of religious innovation and dissent known to diverse ages and cultures (Lewis 1971: 18–126; Weber 1963: 46–59). Although Fish approved of the initial phase of the revival for its uplifting effect and for its impact on

[5] Separates withdrew mainly from the Congregational churches to form bodies of true believers who could demonstrate that they had experienced authentic rebirth. Controversy developed among Separates over the propriety of infant baptism (pedobaptism), and after 1749, many joined Separate Baptist congregations, because of their belief that only the adult reborn were deserving of baptism. Some New Light congregations, including the Narragansett Church, practiced mixed communion of both infant and adult baptism.

church membership, he turned against it when its radical potential came into the open. In a series of nine sermons, which he delivered to the remnant of his North Stonington congregation, Fish recounted the history of the Great Awakening in his parish and outlined his reasons for opposing Separate and Separate Baptist belief and practice. In his opinion, Satan had taken advantage of the enthusiasm to introduce false teaching and thereby divide the Standing churches: "satan by his subtlety, beguiled many religious people, (at a time when there was a glorious work of God begun and going on,) by filling them with a *false spirit*, and making them *believe* that 'twas the *Spirit of God*" (Fish 1767: 129) . Fish particularly disliked the populist idea that any uneducated lay person could claim to be a minister simply on the basis of an internal call:

... learned teachers, though never so pious and faithful, are despised and fled from; and common labourers, even void of common learning, preferred before them,—taken from the field, for which alone they are properly fitted, and set up as pastors and teachers of the people. (Ibid. 86)

... 'tis well known, that the generality of the *baptist churches*, in our part of the world, are poorly furnish'd with *teachers*; both in respect to *learning, knowledge*, and *abilities*: for want of which they are in imminent danger of corrupting the scriptures, by wrong constructions, as well as degrading the office by low and empty performances. (Ibid. 101)

Being a traditional Puritan who valued patience, instruction, and order, and who felt instinctive caution with regard to religious emotionalism, Fish opposed the more expressive aspects of Separate ritual and mistrusted conversions that occurred suddenly in the revival meeting:

THEY paid a great regard to *visions*, or *trances*; in which some would lie for many hours: and on their coming out, or coming to themselves again, would tell of wonderful things,—that they saw, it may be, *heaven* or *hell*, and such and such persons, (if dead), there; or (if alive,) going to one or t'other of those places. . . .

IN their religious conduct, they were influenced rather by *inward impressions*, than by the plain word of God. . . . Neither ministerial advice, nor parental counsel . . . were any weight with them, compared with an IMPRESSION. (Ibid. 139-40)

For when these outcries of *distress* or transports of joy, took place among the people, and had a powerful effect upon their bodies, the good man [Rev. James Davenport] pronounced them tokens of the *presence* of God, and the power of religion. . . .

But more than *this*,—Not only were these violent agitations of body, declared to be the grand tokens of the divine presence and power, but what was still more dangerous, those persons that passed immediately from great distress to great joy . . . were instantly proclaimed *converts*. . . . Whereas . . . *numbers* of such *converts*, in a little time, returned to their old way of living,— were as carnal, wicked, and void of Christian experience, as ever they were. (Ibid. 117-18)

From Fish's point of view the New Light Separates were too confident in mistaken convictions and misrepresented the Bible as a result of their poor training and their faith in revelation and other forms of direct religious knowledge. Although he regretted his own occasional despondency and felt that he sometimes lacked an awakening touch in his preaching, Fish never retreated from an opportunity to challenge the errors he perceived in Separate and Separate Baptist belief.

In addition to his regular duties as the pastor of the North Stonington Congregational Church, Fish devoted much time during the latter half of his career to the education and religious instruction of the Stonington Pequot and the Narragansett of Charlestown, Rhode Island.[6] In this

6 Fish depended upon his ministerial salary as well as upon "benefactions" (firewood, food, candles, seed, etc.) from his congregation for subsistence (Fish 1739-70). Dissension and separation in his par-

Indian work he encountered many of the same problems that had earlier disrupted his English parish, for the Pequot and Narragansett also favored Separate views. From 1757 until his death in 1781, he preached among the Stonington Pequot and for many years looked after their school as a representative of the Company for Propagation of the Gospel in New England and parts adjacent in America (the New England Company) and as a commissioner for the Society in Scotland for Propagating Christian Knowledge. The Pequots, he complained in a letter to the Boston commissioners of the New England Company in 1762, preferred Separate preaching to his own, in this case the preaching of Narragansetts from Rhode Island:

... the Number of Indians attending, at different Lectures, is *various*. Sometimes a number of them was either *hunting*, or at a distance upon then needfull Occasions, or at home Sick, Lame, etc., While some, indeed, were absent, through Sloth and Carelessness. But the principal Cause, I apprehend, has been their great Fondness for the *Indian* Teachers and their Brethren, (Seperates,) from the *Narragansetts*, who were *frequently*, if not *constantly*, with *Our Indians*, or in the Neighborhood, the same day of *My Lectures*, unless I purposely shifted the Time. For these Narragansetts would but Seldom think it proper to *hear Me*: Which tended to Scatter *my* Indians. ... Some of them, especially the Chief Speakers, (from Narraganset,) could not *read* a Word in the Bible. (Fish 1762)

Fish criticized Indian Separates for the same reasons that he did their English brethren—they attributed importance to impressions (trances, visions) over scriptural knowledge, their clergy were poorly trained, they were unduly self-assured in their belief in their own conversion, and overly

ish had weakened the basis of this support, and he probably needed the additional income from Indian missionary work to support his household.

judgmental of the "letter learned" and "hireling" clergy and all others whom they considered to be unconverted. To expose their mistakes and show them a better path, Fish prescribed schools where Indians could learn to read, and determined that a great deal of patience and understanding would be necessary on his part.

In the fall of 1765, Fish visited the Narragansett to discuss the possibility of beginning a school and mission on their reservation and was encouraged by their friendliness and interest in the project. The commissioners of the New England Company, having heard from Fish of his favorable reception among the Narragansett, invited him to initiate a missionary program that would include monthly religious lectures and the creation of a permanent school. With the Indians' endorsement Fish recommended Edward Deake, an Englishman who already had been instructing the Narragansett since June 3, 1765, to be their teacher. The commissioners agreed to pay Fish's salary and expenses and to provide for the construction and maintenance of the school as well as for Deake's wages. The tribe eventually gave a parcel of land near Cocumpaug, or Schoolhouse Pond, for the schoolhouse, which also was to serve as Deake's home.

Weather, health, and personal factors permitting, the elderly parson tried to visit the Narragansett community once monthly for about ten years to inspect school affairs, to preach, and to visit the Indian Church and various Indian homes. The journey, between fifteen and nineteen miles each way, depending upon the route, often took two full days, and he would lodge overnight with prominent English friends who lived near the reservation, such as the Reverend Joseph Park, Colonel Christopher Champlin, or Dr. Joshua Babcock.[7]

[7] Although Fish had religious differences with Park during the Great Awakening, he participated in Park's ordination in 1742, and

THE NARRAGANSETT

The population of the Narragansett community visited by Fish in 1765 was around 350 persons. Most of them made a living by farming, fishing, shellfishing, hunting, and woodcutting in their wooded homeland by the sea in Charlestown, Rhode Island. Although Fish spoke with them only in English (unlike the Mayhews of Martha's Vineyard, he apparently spoke no Indian dialect), many probably spoke Narragansett among themselves.[8] Their homes ranged from the eighteenth-century English-style farmhouses of the Sachem's family to the modest frame houses and traditional wigwams of the common folk.[9]

By the early to mid eighteenth century the Narragansett and many other northeastern Indian groups were becoming deeply acculturated into colonial society, and the Awakening affected them along with thousands of other Americans of European and African backgrounds. The majority of the tribe converted to Christianity in 1743 during the height of the itinerant phase of the revival and after Davenport's visit to the Stonington area. At first they merged with the

---

they seem to have gotten along comfortably in their later years. Their Harvard backgrounds and the fact that Park's church had also undergone separations gave them much in common (Fish 1743; Shipton 1945, VII: 415-21; 1951, VIII: 419).

8 By mid eighteenth century most Narragansett could speak English, although one woman who testified in court in 1753 required an interpreter (Champlin Papers 1753). Ezra Stiles recorded a vocabulary list of forty-five items from a Narragansett in 1769 (Cowan 1973: 7-13). Usher Parsons wrote in 1861 that Narragansett had "ceased to be a spoken language in the tribe for nearly half a century" (Parsons 1861: iii). Thomas Commuck and Albert Gatschet recorded short vocabularies in 1855 and 1879 respectively (Commuck 1859: 291-98; Gatschet 1973: 14).

9 For a description of two Western Niantic wigwams seen by Stiles in 1761, see Sturtevant (1975: 437-44).

English New Light congregation of the Reverend Joseph Park of Westerly, Rhode Island, but soon separated from Park's ministry to form an independent Narragansett Church in the heart of the reservation under their own minister, the Reverend Samuel Niles. Niles, an illiterate, was ordained by Indian brethren without the support of neighboring English clergy. By identifying with the Separate movement the Narragansett converts aligned themselves with some groups and not others within the larger society—specifically with those that shared their position near the bottom and edges of the social order. The Sachem and his family did not belong to Niles's church for they, along with most well-to-do planters of this region, had ties with the Church of England. Although the Narragansett New Lights participated in and internalized many aspects of colonial culture, they also remained a distinct current in that larger stream. This distinctiveness is apparent in their conversion for they selected precisely the form of Christianity that most resembled their ancestral religion. As New Lights they maintained an Indian emphasis on visions, on the spoken over the written word, and on religious leadership that derived its authority from an internal calling as opposed to formal education.[10]

The social forces that accounted for deepening divisions between rich and poor in English colonial society had long affected the Narragansett and other Indian populations in southern New England. Wealthy planters and those with too little land looked to the Narragansett country as an area

[10] For a more detailed account of the social and religious dimensions of Narragansett conversion in the Great Awakening and additional sources on this subject, see Simmons (1979a: 25-36; 1982). Joseph Park, who converted the Narragansett, wrote an account of his experiences which appears in Thomas Prince's *The Christian History...* (1744: 201-11; 1745: 22-28).

where they could expand their holdings. In 1709, in an effort to protect himself and his people from the land-hungry English, the Sachem Ninigret II of the combined Narragansett and Niantic people quitclaimed to Rhode Island colony all Indian lands except a sixty-four square-mile tract in Charlestown, which the colony agreed to oversee as a permanent reservation (Committee of Investigation 1880: 26-28). Despite the 1709 agreement to protect reservation property, the Sachems often found it possible to sell tribal land to repay their personal debts. They had sold so much land for this reason that by 1765, when Fish began his mission, many Narragansett feared they would lose everything.

In 1759 the Sachem Thomas Ninigret persuaded the Rhode Island General Assembly to repeal all laws that limited the sale of reservation land, in order to pay his enormous personal debts (Bartlett 1861, VI: 221).[11] As one farm after another passed from Indian to English hands, a large number of Narragansetts petitioned the General Assembly to prevent the Sachem from selling more acreage without the joint consent of the tribal members and the General Assembly, and the Assembly temporarily forbade Ninigret to do so (Arnold 1896: 18-20). Ninigret protested that he was under financial pressure from many lawsuits, that the land was legally his to sell, and that he always had taken good care of those Indians under his protection (Arnold 1896: 21-25; Flick 1925, IV: 152-60; Hamilton and Corey 1953, XI: 406-8). Two factions are clearly evident within the Indian community at this time. The first included the Sachem and his dependents. The second consisted of common people and a leadership composed of Niles, John

11 Detailed accounts of Ninigret's finances from 1751 to 1757 are in the Champlin Papers in the Rhode Island Historical Society Library (Champlin Papers 1751-57).

Shattock, Tobias Shattock, John Shattock, Jr., Ephraim Coheis, and others who lived on the reservation, who opposed the Sachem, and who were affiliated with the Narragansett Church.

In an effort to reach a compromise between the factions, the General Assembly appointed a committee in 1763 to determine which tracts were used by the Sachem and which were used by the tribe as a whole, and to provide tribal members with a deed to the land they claimed (Arnold 1896: 20-21). The committee did not complete its task, mainly because they could find no specific areas that had been set off for the tribe as a whole (they found many tracts used by particular individuals and families), but also because the Sachem's supporters did not want their land divided off from his and because of disagreement regarding the disposition of large areas of common swamp and woodland (Arnold 1896: 25-26; Bartlett 1861, VI: 401-2; Hamilton and Corey 1953, XI: 237-38). Unable to obtain satisfaction from the Rhode Island government or to prevent the Sachem from selling their best farms, members of Niles's faction retained a lawyer, Matthew Robinson, of Kingston, Rhode Island, and sought allies outside the sphere of Rhode Island politics. In 1764 two Narragansett visited Sir William Johnson of New York, who was the Crown's superintendent of relations with the Indians of the northern colonies. In their papers, prepared by Robinson, the Narragansett explained that they were loyal subjects who had often fought for the King, and that the Rhode Island Assembly would not protect them from the Sachem's violations of the 1709 agreement (Flick 1925, IV: 587-95; Hamilton and Corey 1953, XI: 405-14). The Reverends Eleazar Wheelock of Lebanon, Connecticut, and Matthew Graves of New London, Connecticut, also wrote Johnson in behalf of the aggrieved faction, whose interests they thoroughly supported. Despite numerous compelling appeals by Robinson, Wheelock, Graves, and the Indians, Johnson advised the Narragansett to settle the dispute amongst themselves and chose not to intervene because they were under the authority of a colonial government and were not an independent tribe.

When Fish arrived at the reservation in the fall of 1765, Niles's followers were unhappy because the Rhode Island Assembly after many delays had finally rejected a petition by Niles and Ephraim Coheis (or Coheys), which would have restrained the Sachem (Flick 1925, IV: 659-63). The Indians concluded that justice could not be had under the Rhode Island government because some of its members were among the Sachem's major creditors. Robinson summarized their predicament in 1765 in a second appeal to Johnson:

... agreeable to your hint in the Postscript of your Letter, I continued my Addresses to our Genl. Assembly to get the Affair ended in this Government, but to no Purpose: for after many Continuances, that Court thought proper in their Session last Febry entirely to Vote out my Clients' Petition ... without further Restricting Tom the Sachim from Selling Lands; by which means he is left to his own Will, and I am informed has sold two fine Farms Since. . . .

Perhaps you may wonder Sir at the Conduct of our General Court; but it is easily Accounted for, when it is Considered that two of the Members of that Court were Creditors for Tom ... and that many others (People of Influence) are his Creditors ... by whose means the poor honest Petitioners Address was thrown out.... My Clients desire me to acquaint you, Sir, that their Sachem *Tom* has taken away their fields, and Meadows from them, and given some to one, and Sold some to others.—He has also taken away from them two Saw Mills which they built themselves,—that by Selling away their Meadows they are deprived of getting to the Salt Water for fishing, the Wayes they had ever used time out of mind.—that about forty Acres of their land granted to the Royal Society for a Church of England, he suffers Colonel Champlin, or some of his family to keep possession of. . . . (Hamilton and Corey 1953, XI: 641)

Niles, John Shattock, and many of their group then attempted unsuccessfully to depose Ninigret in 1766, for, among other reasons, refusing to be advised by the tribe and for wasting valuable lands (Arnold 1896: 57-60; Flick 1927, V: 152-54) . Their most demoralizing setback came in 1767, when the General Assembly appointed a committee to sell as much Indian land as would be necessary to settle all of Ninigret's debts (Bartlett 1861, VI: 533) . Having tried and failed to obtain effective allies outside Rhode Island colony (Johnson, Wheelock, Graves, and by now, Joseph Fish) , Tobias and John Shattock, Jr., sailed to England to persuade King George III and others to intervene in their behalf. The voyage proved fruitless, and Tobias died of smallpox in Edinburgh in 1768.

Meanwhile the General Assembly continued to sell Indian property until all Ninigret's debts were paid in 1773, four years after the Sachem's death. When Ninigret died, Niles's group petitioned the assembly to abolish the Sachemdom and replace it with a council to be composed mainly of their supporters. They subsequently agreed to support Thomas's sister, Esther, who succeeded as Queen Sachem in 1770 (Bartlett 1862, VII: 17-18; Narragansett Indians No. 21, 1770) . Although the assembly forbade further Indian land sales after Ninigret's debts had finally been paid, a great deal of moral and material damage had been done. The Narragansett had suffered through more than a decade of governmental indifference to their legitimate grievances and saw their best lands and the fruits of their labor slip away with no compensation, despite their vigorous efforts to work through the colonial court and to seek the aid of influential patrons. Ninigret's lifestyle had been costly to his people.[12]

Fish came to the Narragansett at a time when the church faction most needed him. They had learned to appreciate the usefulness of literacy in conducting their legal affairs and were desirous of a school for their children. They undoubtedly saw him as an ally in their attempts to establish a political network above the heads of the Rhode Island Assembly and speedily enlisted him in their campaign. Throughout his mission Fish worked mainly with Niles's group, whereas the Sachem's followers, perhaps more secure with the support of the local English gentry, showed less interest in his mission and in the school. Fish was aware of the practical goals that Niles and the Shattocks hoped to achieve in accepting his mission, and he willingly helped them by listening to grievances and writing letters in their behalf. He also wished for an end to their political difficulties with the Sachem so that they could concentrate without distraction on education and religious reform. Fish's primary motivations were more religious than prac-

[12] Some Narragansetts emigrated to Brothertown, New York, in 1775 and after 1830, to Brothertown, Wisconsin, where land was more abundant (Love 1899: 223-25, 320-21). Others moved as far away as Michigan, Kansas, North Dakota, and California (Campbell and La Fantasie 1978: 80; Morgan 1870: 219n; Munro-Fraser 1880: 324). The remainder lived on or near the reservation in Charlestown where many of their descendants live today. In 1880 the State of Rhode Island dissolved the tribal government, purchased the remaining 922 acres of reservation, and compensated 324 people of Narragansett ancestry for the sale (Campbell and LaFantasie 1978: 80). The Narragansett Church (rebuilt in 1859), with its accompanying Powwow grounds and cemetery, remains the religious and social center of the Southern Rhode Island Narragansett community, which consists of about 400 persons. For more complete accounts of Narragansett history since 1776 see Boissevain (1975), Campbell and LaFantasie (1978: 67-83), and Simmons (1978: 190-97).

tical, however, and sprang from the theological warfare begun in the Great Awakening. He set out to reclaim the souls that Satan had taken many years earlier when the Narragansett separated from Joseph Park's congregation to follow the ministry of Samuel Niles.[13]

[13] Being at first a moderate New Light who initially supported the revival and then recoiled from it, Fish was severely critical of most aspects of Separate belief and practice. The title *Old Light on Separate Ways* refers to the antirevival perspective through which he viewed Indian Separates during his later years.

Diary and Correspondence,
1765 - 1776

Revd. J. Fish to Docr. Sewel.[1]

[Written after September 18th, 1765][2]

To Doctor Sewal,

Revd. and Hond. Sir, My late Journey to the Narragansetts, and Conversation with the Indians there, has made me further acquainted with their Circumstances than ever I was before; and opend Such an affecting View of their peculiar Situation, especially on Religious Accounts, that I thought it might, in Some Measure, Serve the Redeemers Intrest, to Acquaint You more particularly therewith, and offer my Sentiments thereby than I have done, in my Letter to the Commissioners.

They, These Indians, are not only Numerous, and planted on A large Tract of Land, beyound my Thought: but Many of them Industrious—Dwell in comfortable Houses and have Things about them. They seem to be a hospitable people—Kind and Free of what they have: And, for Indians, a good deal Respectfull. The Heads of Their Tribe who Met to discourse Me, (which I believe were not much short of Twenty,) Appeard to be grave, Solid and Thinking Men, conducting themselves With Discretion.

A goodly Number of them, Men and Women, Are religiously Disposd; and hopefully Retain a good Measure of Serious Impressions of Truth, from the painfull Labours of the Revd. Mr. Park, when they were Under his Care and attended his Ministry. By what I observd, They give a Decent and Devout Attention to every Branch of Worship, Whether at Table, or in public Assembly—Seem tender and Very Susceptible of Impressions, from Truths, peculiarly intresting.[3] And, must confess, by the Small experience I had of their Temper, They appeard to be of a More teachable Disposition, than I expected; (knowing by long acquaintance, the Self-sufficiency of a Seperate Spirit;) For they Seemd to hear Well my pressing upon them the Necessity of a Preachers knowledge of the Scriptures, and of trying all Doctrines, Spirits and Feelings, by *that* Standard. And also Seemd to take in good part, My Recommending to them a greater Freedom and Society with the Standing Ministers and Churches in Neighbouring Towns—That they might have the Benefit of their Assistance, in all Religious Matters.

But After all, The poor unhappy People are So Leavend with a Seperate Spirit and Notions, that I fear their Zeal of God is (in Some aspects,) not According to knowledge. Though, I charitably Suppose, there are numbers of persons among them truely gracious, yet being so Unskillfull in the Word of Rights, and out of the Way of better Instruction, I fear they are not likely to grow in Grace and in the true knowledge of Our Lord J. Cht.

They left Mr. Parks Church and Ministry, I think, about the time that one Deacon Babcock and others fell off from the Standing Churches, and Set up for Teachers about 15 or 20 Years ago:[4] And Were for Some time, Under the Inspection and Influence of Said Mr. *Babcock,* a Seperate Baptist Teacher; till most of them took Offence at his Conduct, in Ordaining an Indian over them, that was not Agreable to the Body of the Tribe.

Upon Which Some of the Indian Brethren (as Im informd) not in any Office, took and ordaind one Samel. *Niles* their Pastor, And he has been their Minister ever Since, for a Number of years: preaching, Administing the Supper, Baptism, and Marriage.[5]

This Niles, (Who I have known Some Years,) is a Sober Religious Man, of Good Sense and great Fluency of Speech;

and know not but a very honest Man. Has a good deal of the Scriptures by heart, and professes a Regard for the Bible. But his unhappiness is this, He *cannot read a Word,* and So is wholly dependant Upon the (too Seldom) Reading of others: Which exposes him, (doubtless) to a great deal of Inacuracy in useing Texts of Scripture, if not to gross Mistakes in the Application of them. And as hereby, (I conclude,) very Much upon the *Spirit* to teach him *Doctrine* and *Conduct,* he is in imminent danger of leaving *The Word,* for the Guidance of *Feelings, Impressions, Visions, Appearances* and *Directions* of Angels and of Christ himself in a Visionary Way. An Instance, of which I have heard of in his ordaining one Indian.

I dont learn that They Are Visited and Instructed by Any english Ministers; Unless it be now and then *One* of the Seperate Stamp.[6] I have not heard of any One of our regular Standing Ministers, being among them for Many Years: which perhaps is a Faulty omission, if they Woud be Willing to *hear* us. Which Indeed I thought they would *not,* till their Freedom to hear *Me* the Other Day, Attended with Expressions of Approbation, and Requests from Some that I'd Visit and *preach* to them Again, Convincd Me that the Door is open, much Wider than I imagind.

Im inclind to think that they are within the reach of Instruction and capable of being corrected in their religious notions, and Set right (at least greatly Mended,) in their Gospel Order, if due pains were usd, and proper Measures taken.

This woud doubtless be the most easily and effectually done, by a faithfull and prudent Missionary Sent among them, Who Should be to their liking. But I apprehend the present Times wont admit of any Such Attempt: as it might look like, (at least be taken for,) a Superceding of their Minister *Niles,* or Some way Lessening his Influence and authority—which, I Suppose Neither *He* nor *They* would relish the Thought of.

Another Method to help them, might hopefully be, by Some Neighbouring Minister, or Ministers (who Shoud be to their good Acceptance, if Such coud be found, Visiting of them and preaching to them, frequently, Taking a little time and pains by Way of free Conversation, on Religious Matters.

Or if the Honourable Commissioners Shoud think proper to Desire their Teacher *Niles,* to come and make them a Visit at Boston, They Might, by free Conversation, hopefully, assist him greatly, in Religious Matters.

The *Report* of the Indian Committee, Who Went down with a Petition for a Schoolmaster, (containing accounts of the favourable Acceptance and kind Treatment they met with,) has raisd the Commissioners So high in the Esteem of the Indians that their Influence over them must needs be Very Considerable; and, I imagine, that They have now in hand a Singular Advantage, in Some Way that their Wisdom may direct, to Serve their best Intrest to good purpose.

The poor people are not fit to be left alone, Not being Equal to the Important affair of Conducting their Religious and ecclesiastical Matters, agreable to Gospel Order. They Want Instruction, Guidence, Counsell. But the most difficult Undertaking to administer it.

I apprehend they cant bear to be told their Errors, and Mistakes in Any *direct* way of Speech. Father Sam, (as they Call him—Their Teacher Niles,) I suppose cant endure to be told, off hand, that his Ordination twas not According to Gospel Order, though ordain, not by the Church, (for I dont learn there was Any Formed), nor by the Presbytery, As the Gospel Directs, But only by a few Individual Professing Christian Indians. Nor will Any of them, (I imagine,) bear to be told, that the Spirit (which They think they have,) is a Safe and Sufficient Guide, Without the Scriptures, And So of *many* Enthusiastic Notions which I Suppose they have. They cant bear to be told, *Directly* that These are *Errors.* This would be too Strong meat. I apprehend They must be told, What is *Truth—Truth* opposite to their Errors, not mentioning *them. Be shown* the *right Way;* passing by the *wrong* at least for a While,) Unnoticd. So that Turning their *Eyes,* and keeping them fixd for a While, Upon *Right Objects,* they May, of themselves take up a good liking to them; and either lose Sight of the *False,* or Gradually See that they were forreign to Truth. And So with respect to all their Errors, Say little or nothing about their wrong ways, but take them by the Hand, put them into and lead them in Right *paths,* till they get a good liking to *these,* and they'll of Course leave the old, and by and by See the Danger of them. These Candi[d] Sentiments I submit to your Correction. The Indians will know that Ive writ you. And they may likely be Jealous (Jealousy being deeply rooted in their Nature,) Jealous, that I've writ Something to their Disadvantage, though I mean Nothing but their best good. If you See it needfull to tell them any thing of the Contents of Mine to you, tell them (as you may truely,) that I have writ you with the highest Friendship to their best Intrest.

....

JOSEPH FISH

Fish papers, Manuscript Collections of the Connecticut Historical Society.

1 Reverend Joseph Sewall (1688-1769) was pastor of Boston's Old South Church, a corresponding member of the Society in Scotland for Propagating Christian Knowledge, and one of the commissioners

appointed by the Company for Propagation of the Gospel in New England and the parts adjacent in America (Sprague, 1857, 1: 278-80).

2 Although this letter was not dated, it was written over a brief and unrelated letter to Fish from Joshua Stoddard of Newport, R.I., dated September 18, 1765. The content of the Fish to Sewall letter suggests that it was written in November or December, 1765, when Fish first began his Narragansett journeys, and before he received word of the commissioners' January 1, 1766, decision to support his mission. Apparently a copy written by Fish for his personal records.

3 According to an account of the Narragansett Church written about this time by a schoolmaster, Samuel Drake, who lived among them for fourteen years: "there are seventy real christians . . . about sixty of them have entered into covenant with God and one another, as a church of Christ, and are determined to follow the lamb of God whithersoever he goes . . . they are also agreed in the articles of faith contained in the apostles creed . . . on *Tuesday, Thursday* and *Saturday* evenings, they constantly meet together to sing and pray to God . . . in their devotions, their affections seem to be surprisingly drawn out . . . they are not fond of receiving any into church fellowship, but such as can give some good account of their being born again, renounce their heathenish practices, subject themselves to the ordinance of baptism, and embrace the above articles of faith . . . they steadily maintain religious worship in their families . . . once in four weeks, they have a meeting on the *Thursday,* preparatory to the communion . . . on the Lord's day following, they celebrate the Lord's supper . . . at certain sacramental seasons, he has thought that the Lord Jesus seemed as it were to be evidently set forth before them" (Beatty 1768: 106-7). The Narragansett Church was also linked with other nearby congregations of Indians: the Mohegan, the Pequot of Groton and Stonington, the Western Niantic, and the Montauk, all of whom converted in the Great Awakening. These groups had occasional communion with the Narragansett, and Niles administered communion to the Indian congregations at Groton and Mohegan (Ibid. 108-9; Dexter 1901, I: 233).

4 Stephen Babcock (1706-75), a native of Westerly, R.I., was a deacon in Joseph Park's congregation. In 1750 he separated from Park's group to form the Church of Christ in Westerly and Stonington in Union, known also as the Hill Church. According to Park: "Babcock did not preach or exhort before he left them, nor was [he] disciplined for that. But that he was overbearing and censorious in Chh. Matters, reflecting on Mr. Parks and the Brethren. For this the Chh. talked with him—which he resented, etc. At length he had a Vision and call from Heaven to preach the Gospel (not to a par-

ticular Chh.) but to strange Nations" (Dexter 1901, I: 233-34 n; see also, Biographical Cyclopedia 1881: 112-13).

5 Ezra Stiles recorded Niles's account of the separation and early formation of the Narragansett Church, as well as some observations on Niles's character, in his diary for May 8, 1772: "This Forenoon I was visited by *Samuel Niles* an Indian of Narragansett AEt. 66. He told me that he was formerly a Communicant in Mr. Parks Congregational Church in Westerly, where he was baptized by Sprinkling. Here he was dealt with for exhorting in the Congregation: upon which he and about a hundred Indians withdrew i.e. the chief body of the Narragansett Tribe which was Christianized. They built a new Meetinghouse 25 feet square: and spontaneously gathered themselves (above twenty Brethren in number) into a Church or agreed to walk together as such. Mr. Stephen Babcock a Deacon of Mr. Parks Church had also separated, and became an Elder among the Separates a mixture of Baptists and Pædobaptists, and was ordained I think by some baptist Elders. There was an Indian from Groton of the Remnants of the *Pequot* Tribe, who came and preached at Narragansett; and he was by the Laying of hands of Elder Babcock and others ordained Elder of this Indian Church; his Name was James Simon or Simon James. But about half a dozen Brethren adhering to him, he and his Adherents met in a private house; to these he administered Baptism and the Lord's Supper, for 3 or 4 years and then removed.

At the same time Samuel Niles carried on in the Meetinghouse; and at length about 15 Brethren who refused Simon, united and called Samuel. But as none of even the Separate Elders would ordain him; the Church chose and appointed three Brethren Indians to ordain him. They began Exercise in the Meetinghouse about noon and held it till near sunset. The 3 Brethren laid their Hands on Samuel Niles, and one of them viz Wm. 'Choise or Cohoize or Oc-Hoyze prayed over him and gave him the charge of that Flock: during which such a Spirit was outpoured and fell upon them (as he expresses it) that many others of the Congregation prayed aloud and lift up their hearts with prayers and Tears to God. This continued for a long Time above half an hour or nearer an hour:—the white people present taking this for Confusion were disgusted and went away. Afterwards they sang and were dismissed. Ever since he has ministered there in holy Things, *preaching, baptizing*, and *breaking bread*. He himself was baptized a second Time, and this was by plunging, and I think by an Indian not an Elder. Yet he professes to hold it indifferent: and it was agreed that baptist or pædobaptist principles and practices should be no Term of Communion. Accordingly

Samuel baptizes both Infants and Adults, and the latter by Sprinkling or plunging, as any are persuaded in their own Minds.... Samuel Niles *cannot read.* It seems extraordinary that such an one should be a Pastor. He is however acquainted with the Doctrines of the Gospel, and an earnest zealous Man, and perhaps does more good to the Indians than any White Man could do. He is of an unblameable Life as to Morals and Sobriety. He has very great Influence over the Indians.... To give him a better Idea of Things I took him into my Study and shewed him a terrestrial Globe, which he had never seen before. I told him he might believe the World a Flat if he pleased.... He said of his own accord he believed it was round like a Ball" (Dexter 1901, I: 232-33).

Being puzzled by the difficulty of choosing between their ministers Niles and Simon, a group of Narragansett converts wrote the Canterbury, Connecticut, Separate Church, for assistance: "We have been in Search of a Pastor till many of us is Lost in the Wilderness; for our Evidences Cross each other, some for James Simon and some for Samll. Niles" (Walker 1897: 119.) For additional background regarding Park's church, Babcock, and the conversion and separation of the Narragansett, see Backus (1871, II: 510-11), Denison (1878: 79-81, 100-3), Gilman (1869: 516-27), Goen (1962: 90-92, 231-32), Love (1899: 191-94), McLoughlin (1979, I: 264n), Parke (1872: 323-27), Prince (1744: 201-10; 1745: 22-28), Shipton (1945, VII: 415-21), and Simmons (1979a: 25-36; 1982).

6 Reverend Matthew Graves, Episcopal parson of New London, Connecticut, had recently visited the Narragansett. He wrote on June 3, 1765, that he had traveled to Charlestown "at their request...and preached to them and given them the best advice I could as a minister and a friend" (Arnold 1896: 48).

Rev. Andrew Eliot DD on Indian affairs to Rev. Jos. Fish[1]

Boston—Jan:2: 1765—

REVD. AND DR. SIR

Your's of the 19 December I received, I was absent when it came and did not know of the Bearer's So Sudden departure or I Should have wrote by him. It gives me great pleasure to hear of your visit to Narragansett, and acceptance with the Indians there. I am Surprised to find So large a number of Indians left without any other instruction than, as it Seems, these have had. I am but lately come among the Commissioners; but I conclude from your account that it must be owing to the Separating Spirit which has been among them, which made them unwilling to hear. I cannot but hope Providence is opening a door of Special service to you, and that you will be an instrument of turning them from their wild notions in Religion. I am quite pleased and So were the Commissioners with the whole of your Letter (for according to the Liberty you gave me I communicated it to them). I cannot but think you have Stated their case with great Judgment and have hit upon the only proper method of conducting towards them. I am Sorry, their Minister is So poorly furnished for his work, and is troubled with Such idle dreams; can we expect much good from Such an one, who will lead them from the Sacred oracles to his own whims and imaginations, if they are no worse? However I entirely agree with you that he is to be treated and Spoken of with great tenderness. I was very cautious in all I Said to the Indian who brought your Letter, who Seems a Sensible Man, who I wish was properly instructed. He might be of great service to his Brethren. I cannot See any great advantage to Samel.'s coming to Boston—But few of the Commissioners would take any particular pains, and without a compliment I am persuaded you can do more than any or even all of us. I am Sensible the care of these Indians will bring a great deal of labor upon you; But what can be done? You are Sensible it will not do to Send a Missionary among them though ever So faithful and prudent. If it would, where is the man? God has given you an interest in their affections, and they are disposed to hear you rather than any one else. What can you do in Such a case? Or what can we do but desire you to Spend as much time with them as you possibly can? This I conclude the Commissioners have desired. There was a Meeting yesterday; I was So much engaged another way, that I Should have had no thought of attending had it not been for your Letter. I went and tarried as long as I could and 'till I apprehended we had agreed upon every thing that could be done at present Relative to the Narragansett Indians. If I can be of any service to you or any way promote the best good of the Indians, I shall embrace the opportunity with [. . .]. You will at any time give me pleasure when you favor me with your commands—I heartily wish you the presence of Christ in every part of your work, and am

> with great Respect
> Your Sincere Friend
> and humble Servant
> ANDREW ELIOT

P.S. Mrs. Eliot joins me in Sending our Respects to Mrs. Fish. Please to remember us to Mr. Eells and his good Family when you See them.[2]

Fish papers, Manuscript Collections of the Connecticut Historical Society.

[1] Reverend Andrew Eliot (1718-78) was pastor of the New North Church in Boston and participated in Indian mission work as a commissioner for the Society in Scotland for Propagating Christian Knowledge and the Company for Propagation of the Gospel in New England and the parts adjacent in America (Shipton 1963: 397-428; Sprague 1857, I: 417-21).

[2] Nathaniel Eells (1711-86), the Congregational minister of Stonington, a Harvard classmate and personal friend of Fish (Shipton 1951, VIII: 409-16; Wheeler 1900: 88-89, 362-63).

First Book 1765

Account of Indian Affairs at Charlestown, Narraganset, Rhode Island

Novr. 26. 1765. At the Request of the Commissioners at Boston, per their Vote and Letter, I made a Journey to Charlestown, which took me Two full Days, close attention.

The Male Heads of the Tribe met me at Jno. Shaddicks[1] —found, by their Account, the Body of the Tribe United in earnest desire of a School Set up Among them.[2] They unanimously Agreed on a Spot to erect a School house—[?Freely] promised to do all that they were capable of, towards building Said House, and that they would be helpfull towards Supporting the Schoolmaster, in Labour etc.

Examind Mr. Edwd. *Dake*, an English Man, (Whom the Indians Chose to Teach their Children,) and Judging Him Considerably well accomplished to teach an English School; and also by Intelligence from the Neighbourhood, found him a Man of good Report, as to his Moral Character, I appointed Him their Schoolmaster, to Teach the Indian Youth, (in Said Charlestown,) to read English, write and Cypher: And Allowd him, for Said Service, at the Rate of £24. per Annum, to be paid Quarterly, by the Commissioners at Boston—To Make Trial for one Quarter, or half a Year, and then to Continue in the School, As We Should find mutual encouragement and Satisfaction. Told them, That if the Master Shoud have a Hundred Schollars in his School, or belonging to it and So under his Care, (as Mr. Dake and the Indians Judgd there would be,) Then I woud Influence his Proposal and Request for a Larger

Salary, He Serving with Fidelity and to Satisfaction. And Indeed, that if he Should have a full School (which a much less Number would Make,) And kept it faithfully, finding that he Could not Support himself with the Above Allowance, I woud Favour him with all proper Assistance for a further Consideration. Also, That as Mr. Deke has already kept School Among Said Indians about 4 months, (part of it by my advice,) for which he has had no Valuable Consideration from Indians or any else, I thought it proper he Shoud Apply to the Commissioners, for Allowance for *that* Service, if they Shoud judge it fitting, especially from the Time I advisd him to keep up the School. Heard 4 or 5 of the Indian Boys (who had been under Mr. Dakes Instruction,) *Read* or *Spell*, And found them quite Expert for the Time, a hopefull Evidence of Learning Among them.

Gave the Indians Advice and Direction, Touching their Conduct, relative to the School, and to the Strangers, (of other Tribes, Molattos, etc.) that dwell among them, viz: to behave peaceably and friendly towards them, allowing *their* Children Benefit of the School, if there was Room and the Master Liesure from tending Schollars of their own Tribe. Also, Touching their Religious Conduct, in Many Respects.

Engagd them any needed Assistance, in Obtaining Supply of *Books* for the School, This Fall.

1 John Shattock was a member of Niles's church and a resident of the reservation. His name is spelled variously Shaddick, Shattock, Shaddock, Shadduck, and Shattuck. His sons, John Jr. and Tobias (Toby), were active in the Narragansett Church and in the political struggle against the Sachem.

2 Teachers had been available to the Narragansett prior to this date. Around 1744 Joseph Park employed an Indian woman who taught reading in a wigwam and he later operated a schoolhouse; Samuel Drake who wrote a brief account of the Narragansett taught in the

vicinity for fourteen years prior to 1768; and in 1765, Cornelius Bennett taught for a brief period before his death (Beatty 1768: 106; Guildhall Library Ms. 7952: March 27, 1751; Kellaway 1961: 196-97; Ninegrett 1765; Prince 1745; 27; Tucker 1877: 68).

NOVR. 27. 1765. P.M. Preachd a Lecture to the Indians at Charlestown, at their public Meeting house, To a Considerable Auditory, I judge about 50, the greater part Indians.

Forwarded An Account of their Doings to the Honourable Commissioners . . . .

The Honourable Commissioners for Indian Affairs, at Boston, having Receivd my Account of the State of the Indians at Narraganset, and of my Appointing a Schoolmaster *there*, as in the foregoing pages, passd Several Votes, at their Meeting Jany. 1. 1766, Desiring Me to Direct and Conduct the Affair of Building a Schoolhouse for Said Indians, To preach Lectures to them, as often as I can, (till further Order,) at 6/8 a Lecture, To Charge for my Travel Whenever I go to preach Said Lectures, And To make Account of the Expences I have already been at, in that Affair, (viz: My first Journey,) . . . .

Account of Lectures preachd to the
Narraganset Indians, at the
Request of the Honourable Commissioners Boston.

Date	Lectures and Texts	Indians present	Price
1765			
Novr. 27.	1 Lecture Zech: 9.12	About 50	0.6.8
1766.			
Mar: 5.	2nd Lecture Jer: 23.29.	Storm. 53	0.6.8
Apr. 18.	3rd Lecture Luk: 19.10.	out Town 45	0.6.8
May 14.	4 Lecture Jno. 7.46.	54	0.6.8
July 2d.	5 Lecture 1 Cor: 1.30		
	Abroad-at-Work—	45	0.6.8

Augt. 6.	6 Lecture Cant. 4.1 (30 most out at Work and Some told them I woud not come this Week).	33	0.6.8
Sepr. 3.	7th Lecture Pm. 97.10.	50	0.6.8
			£2.6.8

....

Travel to preach Lectures to the Narraganset Indians, (Including all Special Service and Charges, which *that* Affair necessarily puts me to, viz: about the School and the Building the Schoolhouse, etc.) at 13/4. a Journey, i.e. Sh 20/. each time, Including the Lecture.

Reasons directing my Judgement to Charge Such a Sum, viz:

These Indians are not the proper Subjects of my Care. I tend my Own Indians, their School, Funerals, marriages, Visits etc. Gratis: And have nothing but the Small Reward of 6/8. per Lecture.

Distance, 15 Miles, nearest way, to the Narragansetts— Too much for 1 Day, not to be travelld at All Seasons, and 19 Miles by Post Road—2 good Days Work, with what follows. So that

Time Spent, ordinarily, 2 Days if good Weather: if bad, Sometimes 3 Days.

Business to be done, Building their Schoolhouse, Directing the Affairs of the School, and Church, Settling their Debates, Healing Differences, (The Parties being Strong,) and Such like things, Cost me much *Care*, *Talk* and *Time*. Besides much Writing for them.

Hardship, Am Much exposd for Want of *Suit*able and Seasonable Refreshment.

Expences, in the Wear of Cloths, Horse Tackling and Silesh, the latter only, at common Rate 3/. Besides all

their Entertainment At My House, Time and cumber *there*.
Family, So much left, exposd to Many Difficulties.

Travel, Time and Business, at Each Lecture,
to the Narraganset Indians.

		£ Sh D
1765.		
Novr. 26.	To 1 **Journey,** Examind and appointed Mr. Deake Schoolmaster. Took me 2 days.	0.13.4
1766.		
Mar: 5.	To a 2nd Journey—much Talk and pains with the Indians, to heal their party Differences, on Account of which the Building their School House Stopped. Very stormy—took 3 days.	0.13.4
Apr. 18.	To 3rd Journey—Inspected the Schoolhouse–Directed the Indians in future proceedings–Discoursd them about Appropriating Lands, etc. Wrote a Letter to 'Sqr. Robinson, to prepare an Instrument of Appropriation.[1] Took 2 Days.	0.13.4
May 14.	To 4th Journey—Took Care of the Building—Orderd 4 Windows to be 3 Squares Wide and 5 Ditto high: and So Save 20 Squares. Directed Indians to See that all their Boards were ready etc. Wrote order and Letter to Mr. Pease etc.[2]	0.13.4
July 1 and 2.	5th Journy—Examind the State of the School—about 30 Small Children, in Letters, Ordinarily attending. Indians	0.13.4

Spirited for their Childrens Learning.
Had Conference with Indians, after
Lecture, about the *School House.*
Found them Strong in Resolution to
compleat the Building, When Hurry
of Business was over. Concluded to
wait till I had Advice from the Indian
Council, About drawing for Money
for Boards. Found the Indians firmly
attached to me; as far as coud Discover. Visited the Indians, Tuesday
P.M. and Wednesday A.M. 7 Families.
This Journey Took me 2 Full days.

Aug. 6th   6th Journey—Found the State of the   0.13.4
School much as above, only on the
growing hand, as the Master informd
me. This Journey I performd in one
Day, but found it rather too hard.

Sepr. 3.   7th Journey—The Indians Consulted   13.4
me about the Difficulty Arising on Mr.
Greaves's appointing a New Master.[3]

---

[1] Matthew Robinson (1709-95) was a respected lawyer in Kingston, R.I., who had been representing Niles's faction in its effort to prevent Thomas Ninigret from selling land. The Rhode Island General Assembly appointed him in 1767 to draw up a deed for three acres of land to be executed by Thomas Ninigret for the use of a Narragansett Indian school, but the deed was not finalized until several years later (Bartlett 1861, VI: 534; 1862, VII: 23-24; Biographical Cyclopedia 1881: 105-6; Carpenter 1924: 83, 171; Kimball 1903, II: 400; Narragansett Indians No. 17, 1768; Weeden 1910: 150).

[2] Simon Pease (1695-1769) was a prominent Newport, R.I., merchant and a founder of the Redwood Library and of Rhode Island University—now Brown University (Phillips 1967: 5).

[3] Reverend Matthew Graves (?-1780) was the Anglican pastor of St. James Church in New London from 1748 until 1779 (Caulkins 1895: 445-47; Decker 1976: 57, 243-45; Weis 1936: 95). He requested the Anglican Society for the Propagation of the Gospel in Foreign Parts to

sponsor a school among the Narragansett, but when the society agreed
to do so, the Indians rejected the offer. They resented Graves's choice
of overseer for the school, (?Thomas) Cross, for recently having bought
their best fishing ground from the Sachem. Tobias Shattuck wrote to
William Johnson that "Mr. Graves petitioned home for a school to be
set up among us, it was granted and Mr. Graves, perhaps notwith-
standing that Mr. Cross was an enemy to us, appointed him to have
the care and inspection of it. But as Mr. Cross has proved himself
an enemy to the Indians, they would be glad to have nothing to do
with him" (Arnold 1896: 34). Graves later wrote Johnson to inform
him that "they have rejected my friendship and the Society's Offices
and preferred a canting ignorant enthusiast" (Ibid. 50-51). Whether
Graves was referring here to Edward Deake, or to an Indian choice
for teacher in Graves's newly approved school is not clear. In any
event, the Indian refusal to accept Cross put an end to the Anglican
school project (Flick 1927, V: 220-21; 1928, VI: 58-61).

....

Expences at My house

1765.		£ShD
Novr.	Entertaining Toby Shaddick	0.1.0
Item	Ditto Another Indian	0.0.6
Item	To Writing (and Transcribing,) Two large Letters, 1 to Honourable Commissioners 1 Ditto to private Gentleman.	0.4.0
Item	To Writing to Mr. Deake on Affairs of the School, and to the Indians	0.1.0
1766.		
Jany.	Entertaining Mr. Deake and Toby Shaddick—Dind	0.0.8
Feb: 7.8.	Entertaining Mr. Deake and Horse a Night and part 2 Days.	0.1.6
Feb: 8.	Going to Sqr. Phelps's[1]—viewing our School House—Consulting about Dimensions—Writing Instructions to the Indians about the House etc.	0.2.0

Feb: 24.   Entertainment Samel. Niles—Writing to   0.1.0
the Indians on Difficulty about Timber
etc.

Special Charges

1766.   £ Sh D

Feb: 25.   Entertaining [?*Sach*], *Danel.* and *Sachim.*   0.2.6
Victuals, Drink, Horses, and My Time.
½ Day, on Difficulties about School
House.

Mar: 4.   Ditto Toby Shaddick and Horse, Night   0.2.6
and Day, and My Time in hearing his
account of their difficulties etc.

Mar: 7.   Ditto Samel. Niles—Victuals and Time.   0.0.6

Mar: 10   To Writing 1 Large Letter to Commis-   0.3.00
sioners. 1 Ditto to Mr. Deake and 1 Ditto
to the Indians—All about the Schoolhouse.

Apr. 1.   To Entertaining Mr. Deake and Horse—   0.1.6
Writing Letter to Mr. Pease N. Port, and
1 Ditto to Indians about Schoolhouse—
And My Time.

July 3.   Writing Large Letter to Mr. Oliver, giv-   0.1.6
ing particular Account of Indian Affairs
at Narraganset.[2]

                                            0.11.6
                                            0.11.8
                                        £ 1.3.2

....

1 Probably Dr. Charles Phelps (1732-1808), a resident of Stonington
and "overseer" of Stonington Indians (Dexter 1916: 410; Perkins 1895:
211; Wheeler 1900: 538; Wheeler 1903: 157-58).

2 Andrew Oliver (1706-74) was then secretary to the Massachusetts
General Assembly and commissioners' secretary and treasurer for the

Company for Propagation of the Gospel in New England and the parts adjacent in America (Kellaway 1961: 177-78; McCallum 1932: 302).

To The Revrd. Mr. Jos. Fish / In Stoningtown

Charlestown December the 5th Day AD 1765
The council Belonging to the Narraganset tribe of Indians met togather And give in list of the family's Belonging there unto and number of children Thats fit for Instruction. There appears to be Seventy three family's Viz: Samuel Niles, Jeams Daniel, Jeams Niles, Joseph Geffery, Thomas Lewis, Anthony Wilson, Jeams Cuff, Roger Wobby, Joseph Rogers, Isaac Rogers, Widow Sarah Rogers, widow Margery Hammer, widow Margery Aaron, widow Mary Hammer, Isaac Robins, John Simon, John Daniel, Har. Daniel, William Sachem, widow Margery Hammer, Micael Toby, Jeams Niles Jr., Harry Hazsard, David Phillip, widow Mary Dick, widow Abigal Sampson, widow Hannah Tuhy, widow Elisabeth Robins, widow Abigal Boson, widow Sarah Toby, widow Sarah Quagonus, Stephen Coyhez, widow Hannah Cheets, John Anthony, Thomas Sachem, Anthony Hull, Tobias Coyhez, Charles Anthony, widow Elisabeth Ephraim, Joseph Coyhez, Cosen Joe, widow Sarah Sampson, John Wompy, widow Mary Will., John Shadick, Jeams Robins, Tobias Shadick, Sarah Daniel, William Skesuck, Henry Harry, Christopher Harry, Daniel Harry, Ephraim Coyhez, widow Queen Cate, widow Sarah Tom., Thomas Coyhez, Thomas Paul, Widow Hannah Penny, Joseph Tuhy, Thom. Tuhy, Anthony King, Jeams Wobby, David Skesuck, widow Sarah Potheg, widow Sarah Paul, Samuel Puckey, David

Secator, Jeams Wobby, Jeams Talker, Dinah Paul, Widow Margret Anthony, wd. Hannah Tias, wd. Bash Harry.

The Number of Children that is fit for Instruction appears to Be One Hundred and fifty one, according to the Best Inteligence that I can obtain [of] the tribe. Besides these there Is a considerable Number of mixtures as melattoes and mustees which the tribe Disowns, and Sundry families of Indians which properly Belongs to other tribes.[1]

The tribe is of the oppinion twill answer to Build the School House But 40 feet in Length and 16 feet in Bredth, one Story with a Strait Roof, and the Chimney in the middle with two Smokes etc. We conclude that we Shall want for the use of the School Eight Doz. Spelling Books and three Doz. testaments at present.

I Should Esteem it a favour to Have Some Books containing the catechism agreed on by the Reverend Assembly of Divines at Westminster, And to Have Spelling Books Set forth by Thomas Dilworth Schoolm[aster].[2]

from yr. friend and very Humbe. Ser. Edward Deake

Fish papers, Manuscript Collections of the Connecticut Historical Society.

[1] Population estimates for the Narragansett tribe at this period are variable. Stiles counted 248 people in 1761 and the next year mentions a larger figure of about 600 (Dexter 1916: 54, 114-15). One count of 315, said to have been made by the schoolmaster Samuel Drake around 1766, accords closely with an estimate of little more than 300 made by Stiles in 1765 (Beatty 1768: 106; Stiles 1872: 162). Fish wrote in his July 30, 1766 letter to Nathaniel Whitaker that the population was "more than Three hundred Souls." A census taken a few years later in 1774 records a total of 528 Indians living in Charlestown at that time (Rhode Island General Assembly ... June 1774).

[2] The Assembly of Divines convened at Westminster in 1643-47 approved two catechisms, *The Larger Catechism* and *The Shorter Catechism*, both of which were available in American editions at this time. *The Shorter Catechism* was available in *The New England Primer ...*, which was first published in 1683, and also was available in several editions (Cohen 1977: v-xxvii). Thomas Dilworth's *A New Guide to the English Tongue* was first published in England by Henry Kent

in 1740 and was the most popular and frequently reprinted of many English spelling books produced in the eighteenth century (Alston 1967).

[*Edward Deake to the Reverend Joseph Fish*]

Charlestown the 13th Day of Decemb. AD 1765 Edward Deake, to the Revd. Mr. Jos. Fish, Sendeth Greetings. Grace from God, and peace from the Lord Jesus Christ, be multiplied, to your Soul Amen.

I would Inform your honour, that our School Dayly Increase's: I have Had alrady Fifty three children under my Instruction, and Expect many more. What Gives me the gratest Incouragements is that I find them, in general, Ingenious to Learn. The tribe, In general, appears to be very thankful that their children is Like to Be Educated, and christian knowledge is Likely to be permoted among them. I have Been conversant with the tribe, Especially with the Heads of the Church, and I find they are much Effected with the Lecture you Preached when you was at our town—which may possibly give you Encouragement to vist us again, Sooner then you Expected, when you were at our town, which I Should Esteeme as a previlidge.

from Sr. yr. Very Humble Servt. Edward Deake

I Should Be much obliged to you if you would Help me to Some Cash—my Second Quarter will Be out the first of January, Exclusive of Lost time. I am in haste Sr. yr. hum. Serv.

Edwd. Deake

Fish papers, Manuscript Collections of the Connecticut Historical Society.

To The Revd. Mr. Jos. Fish / in Stoningtown

Charlestown the 18 Day of Decembr. AD. 1765
TO THE REVD. MR. FISH.

Sr. I would give you a full, and Inteligable Accompt, of my School. I Began to Instruct the Indians the third of June. My Number of Schollars was thirty. (The tribe, at that time, was at varience among themselves.) I continued my Instructions among Them, 'till they were united, in the Subject of a School, which was about the 20th of September (Excepting 12 Days I lost, by Sickness). Then was not well gain, and lay by till I Received the First Letter, and then Began the 14th of October, and Have Continued Ever Since, with no Loss of Time. My School has Dayly Increased Ever Since, and is like too. I have this Day 81 Children Under my Instruction; and have had in whole 100. I called the Council of Indians togather (Viz: Saml. Niles, Tobias Shadick, Jeames Daniel, John Shadick, Jeams Niles, Tom. Lewis, Cousin Joe, Ephraim Coyhez) to Inform me of the age of the youths or children. I find them to be mainly Between four and fourteen. I have But one thats twenty years of Age in my School. As to their Learning, there is Seven that Read and writes. The Others are mainly In a tolerable way of Spelling. I have But 15 that Don't know their Letters etc. I have kept School three months, Before I had any Real Incouragement from the Commissioners, as you may See By the above accompt.

From Sr. your Humbe. Servt. Edwd. Deake

P.S. I understand, by Toby, you could hardly Beleave my accompt of Scholars I informed you of. I only Informed you of what I Happen to Have that Day—if you Cannot Beleave me you must Send Somebody that you Can Beleave to take an accomt of them.

Edward Deake

Fish papers, Manuscript Collections of the Connecticut Historical Society.

To the Revd. Mr. Joseph Fish / in Stoningtown

Charlestown the 7 of June AD 1766

REVD. SR.,

I would now Inform you of the present Obstruction, which attends a Speedy dispatch in compleating the *School-House*. Soon after your last visit, the Carpenter called upon the Indians for his *Wages*, to Answer the Demands of an English *Gentleman*, and furnish his Family with the Necessaries of life.[1] The poor *Indians* being unable to Answer his Demand, for want of *money*, the Carpenter was Obliged to Labour else where. The *Indians* being uneasy the House Should Stand, unfit for me to live in, came for *advice*, which I gave as followeth. I think you will find it in your way, to Comply with the *Commissioners* Request in Appropriateing the *House*, and *Land* to the use of a *School*: then Draw an order upon Esqr. *Oliver* for money for Boards, which may Serve to help your Carpenter, and furnish you with Present Necessaries of Life, and set forward your *Building* as usual. This advice was Approved of, by Some of the Heads of the Indians, but the grater part of the tribe opposed it, through fear of being led into a Snare, by the Commissioners, useing this argument: if there was no trick, or Snare laid for us, the Commissioners, would let us have pay for the Boards, before the Instrument was Executed. Further saying, there was formerly Gentlemen in Boston, that tryed to get a Mortegage on our Lands, under pertence of great friendship, and we know nothing to the Contrary but what these Gentlemen has Some Sinister view, and as we have Lost great part of our Land already, by Signing Instruments to please the English, at the Same time understanding Nothing of the Nature of them.[2] I think it Should teach us to be more careful, Lest it Should be with us as it is already with Some of our Bretheren; in Steed of having them Brought up to Learning, Obliged to Bind our Children Servants to the English Creditors, to keep out of Prison, (or Words to the Same efect) .[3]

Upon this I Informed them, that I had Seen all the writing, Relating the School that the Commissioners had wrote, therefore was Confident the Commissioners Had Nothing else in view but their promotion in Christian knowledge. Toby, testifying he Never Saw the Least appearance of any thing in the Commissioners but friendship, which Seemed to yield them Some Satisfaction, and they Still Remain easy and Calm in mind.

If the Indians Should break with the Commissioners, and you, I Shall Despare of ever Seeing that orders, Established among them, which I am now in Hopes of Seing. Therefore according to the best Light I have at Present, beleave 'twould be best for you to visit them as Soon as may be, and Draw an order for Money at Lest; and let the Sequestration of the House, and Land rest a little longer. 'Twill Serve to keep their minds free, and Increase their love toward you, and the most Certainest Method that can be taken, to prepare them to Execute the aforesaid Instrument.

The Indians know Nothing of this Letter. Neither do I

want they Should, if you think my advice is worthy of Notice, that all may appear as your care of them. I am now teaching their Children in the School-House, with but little done to it Since you See it Last. Uncomfortable in the Night season for the Strongest Constitution, but through the Goodness of *GOD*, I've had my Helth beyond my Expectation. But it is otherways with my Wife.

In Grateful Remembrance of Friendship, and *Civility* with Complements to Madm. *Fish*, I am, Sr. yr. Obedent Humle. *Servant.*

Edward Deake

Fish papers, Manuscript Collections of the Connecticut Historical Society.

1 William Welsh, an English neighbor of the reservation; see diary, October 1, 1766.

2 Between 1658 and 1662, Humphrey Atherton of Massachusetts and a company of his associates laid fradulent claim to most of the remaining Narragansett territory. Although the King's Commissioners ruled the claim to be void in 1664, it persisted for many years afterwards. Deake may be referring to this controversy. Accounts of the Atherton mortgage can be found in Burlingame et al. (1925), Arnold (1860, I: 272, 275-76, 378-86), and Leach (1958: 16-17, 23).

3 Indian fears of imprisonment and servitude were not unrealistic (Lauber 1913: 110, 294; Sainsbury 1975: 378-93).

The Rev. Mr. Nathaniel Whitaker in London
To be left at the New England Coffee House[1]

Stonington July: 30. 1766
REVD. AND DEAR SIR:

....

While Such important Steps are taken, to carry the Gospel among the Savages, of far distant Tribes, it may, perhaps, afford *you* and *Friends*, some additional Pleasure to hear that Learning and Religion Are, hopefully, reviving, among some of the Indians near at hand.

Besides the Indian School and Lectures among the Indians of my own Parish, which I've had the Care of for Many Years, At the earnest Request of the Honourable Commissioners Boston, I have for Nine months Past been much engagd for the Indians of King *Ninnegretts* Tribe in Charlestown, Rhode Island, Where there Are above Seventy Indian Families and more than Three hundred Souls, pretty much in a Body together. Authorizd as Above, I appointed them An English Schoolmaster, of good Capacity and well disposd for the Business, (to be Supported by the Commissioners,) Set them up a [?Commodious] Schoolhouse, in which, (though unfinishd,) the Master lives and the School is Steadily kept. He had, last Winter, (in a private house,) above Fourscore Indian Schollars in a day, and about 120 that come to the School, at times, And their Proficiency at Reading and Writing was Very considerable. *That fall* being chiefly calld off the Business, this Summer, he has, of a Smaller Crop, about *Thirty* that generally attend his School and the number is increasing.

I Visit and Preach to them about Once a month. Have a Considerable Assembly of Serious, Attentive Indian Hearers, who profess Satisfaction, beyound my Thought. For they have had Religion Among them these Twenty years, and an Indian Ordaind Minister for a number of years: but they are all of the *Seperate Stamp*,—Very Ignorant:— Scarce any of them able to read a Word,—Unhappily leavind with, yea full of *False Religion*,—tenacious of their wild Imaginations and Visionary things, (Which they cannot bear to hear touchd, though they'll readily hear the Oposite Truths,) And, till now, Set against, at least, mortally afraid of the *Standing* Ministers. So that I must think my Self highly Favourd, by the Respect they Shew to my Person and Regard for my Labours Among them. Am in hopes they will, by little and little, come off from their wild notions, and have a relish for nothing but *Truth.*

Oh that I may have no other View but their best good, And the Redeemers Intrest.

....

JOSEPH FISH

....

Manuscript Collections, Dartmouth College Library.

1 Reverend Nathaniel Whitaker (1732-95), who on December 23, 1765, accompanied the Mohegan Indian minister Samson Occom to England to raise funds for Moor's Charity School (McCallum 1932: 262n; Richardson 1933).

Second Book 1766

Account of Lectures, Travel and Expences, to the Indians at Narragansett

....

OCTR. 1 ... Examind the Indians Account of Boards, now in the Building—School house. Found they amounted to £9.5.6. errors excepted: for which I receivd of Commissioners, and paid the Indians 9.1.00.

Endeavourd to quiet the Uneasiness and Clamour that has arisen, among the English and Indians, on Account of the New Schoolmaster, Appointed by Mr. Greaves. Returnd the Same day, late at night . . . .

OCTR. 29 . . . Indians at work on the Chimney—Gave directions about the Same—Excited them to make the house Comfortable for Master and Children, before Winter. Endeavourd to Compose a Difference between an English Neighbour (Wm. Welsh,) and the Indians, about a Load of Boards, in Partnership between Said Welsh and John Shaddick. Welch Demanded pay, and Chargd the Indians with being not up to their Word; in that he had none of the Money Sent them by Commissioners, though they promised him pay of the first Money that came. I told him Jno. Shaddick had not drawd For pay, for the Boards he put in—That none of the Money I brought belongd to Shaddick, and So that *Welch* had no right to a penny of it —and that none had promisd him but Shaddick, And therefore he did not do right to Charge the rest of the Indians with failing of their Promise . . . .

Novr. 10 . . . Inspected the Building of the Chimney—found it in a good Way. Spent Some time, before Lecture, in discoursing with a Number of Indians, on Religious Matters. Recommended to them the Reading of the Holy Scriptures, publicly, on Lords Days, by the Schoolmaster; as but very few of the old Indians could read a word. Returnd next Day . . . .

. . . Decembr. 8. 1766 . . . enquird about the School House, (holding the Lecture at Jno. Shaddicks,) Informd me they had finishd the Chimney—were underpinning the house, and going on with the Building, fast as they Could.

The School had not been kept, Since they begun the Chimney, (Some Weeks ago) by reason of the house being Unfit to meet in, this cold Weather. James Daniel offerd a Room, in his house, for the Use of the School this Winter: but Some Indians Opposd it, intending Soon, to move the Master and Family, into the School house And keep there.[1] This Intelligence I had from Mr. *Deake* . . . .

[1] James Daniel was more closely allied with the Sachem's faction than with Niles's and Shattock's group; see diary, August 16, 1768.

. . . March 2. 1767. Found the School well kept up—not a Day but Master and Schollars attended their Business. From 28 to 40 Schollars—Common Number 28 or 30—As Many as the Master Can Well Teach. One End of the Schoolhouse Glazd and Somewhat Comfortable, The Other not. Indians intend to put forward the Work, This Spring. Besides Preaching, Read the Scriptures to the Indians and made Some Remarks. After Sermon, The Indians Sung a Hymn in their Way; And then Several of them, very devoutly Exhorted and Stirred up one Another.[1] Had a Very Solemn Meeting, and the Number of Hearers Much larger than ever before . . . .

[1] The principal accounts of Narragansett belief and ritual for this period are those by Samuel Drake (Beatty 1768: 106-9) and Ezra Stiles (Dexter 1901, I: 232-34). The nineteenth-century collection of Indian music by Thomas Commuck, a Brothertown, Wisconsin, Narragansett, may contain some early Narragansett hymns (Commuck 1845).

. . . MARCH 30. 1767. The Bridge (over which I usd to ride,) being gone, went round Shattocks Ware Bridge, (as before, but now,) found many obstructions, by the Way—made me Late;[1] So that many who came to hear preaching were gone, before I got there. Read the 28th Matth: and preachd to a Large Assembly, Supposd to be 150. Am Apt to Think (Though they could not in their moving Posture, after Lecture, easily be numberd,) there were not quite So Many, but likely *more* than 100. Indians Settled their Sacrament the Last Sabbath in each Month: and my Lecture to be the Next Day, i.e. The First Monday, after the Last Sabbath in each Month. After Lecture, Discoursd Largely, with Mr. *Deake* and *Toby, Seperably* and *Together*, About the Danger the Indians, of This Tribe, are in, of coming under Mr. Greaves, N. Londo., and Submitting them to (*Episcopal*) Regulations, By reason of Mr. Greaves's Intresting him Self about their *Lands*—writing to General Johnson, in their Behalf And representing himself, (or So Conducting, as to be thought, by the General,) The very greatest Friend that the Indians have.[2] Toby Informd me, that Mr. *Greaves* offers to Instruct *him* Gratis. *Both* told me that Mr. *Greaves* offers to Let them use the Finest School in the Country—A Master of high Learning—To Teach their Children Latin etc. Talks very finely to them, And pleases them very much.

I advisd Toby and his Brother to Return to Mr. Wheelocks School—To Continue Learning there, To Visit his own Tribe once in 2 or 3 Months, To keep his place in their Council and do them all the Service he Can, while getting his Learning . . . .[3]

1 Shattuck's Weir, a fishing site on the Pawcatuck River in Niantic (Dorrville), R.I., named for an Indian associated with the early history of the place (Denison 1878: 184).

2 Graves first wrote Sir William Johnson regarding Narragansett land problems on June 3, 1765. He observed that: "Their case is truly pitiable and call[s] badly for immediate relief. Their worthless Sachem is daily selling their lands etc., the inhabitants of Rhode Island as well as the neighbors surrounding them are the purchasers. The Assembly I find neglect their complaint and the great men who should prevent their ruin and buy their lands for nothing" (Arnold 1896: 47). In his letter Graves included a list of twenty-nine substantial land sales made by the Sachem between 1758 and 1763 which amounted to a total of 3,274.25 acres (Ibid. 47-49; Flick 1925, IV: 756-58). Again in 1767, Graves wrote Johnson: "Their hardships still increase and within these few last months a very large and valuable tract of land has been purchased from their scandulous Sachem" (Arnold 1896: 50).

3 Mr. Wheelock's School refers to Moor's Charity School in Lebanon, Connecticut, where Reverend Eleazar Wheelock (1711-79) instructed Indian youths from the Narragansett, Mohegan, Montauk, Delaware, Oneida, and other northeastern tribes to become schoolteachers and missionaries among Indians. Tobias and his brother John Shattock, Jr. entered the school in December, 1766, and attended intermittently for almost one year before they returned to Charlestown to aid in the struggle against the Sachem (Lathem 1971: v-x; McCallum 1932: 201-9; McClure and Parish 1811: 277).

. . . APR. 27. 1767. Found the School kept up, but a very few Schollars, just now: the bigger Children gone to work, and the Smaller, for Want of Clothing, or Some Such impediment, not generally Sent; which the Master told me was usually the Case, at this time of Year: but expected more, soon as the Weather was Warmer.

Understood by Mr. Deake that the Indians were well pleasd with Tobys going to Learning—That the Party which held to the Sachem, would do nothing to the Schoolhouse, nor hardly Send their Children to School . . . .

. . . JUNE 1. Found all things quiet—But a Small Number of Schollars, (about 10,) that Attend these Weeks past—More expected Soon. Schoolhouse, and All Other things, much as they Were. Nothing Special for Me to do—Returnd At Night . . . .

. . . JUNE 29. 1767. Found the School kept as usual—13 Schollars. Discoursd largely, after Lecture, With Samel. Niles, Jno. Shattock and James Niles, about the Danger they are in, of loosing their Lands; And What Method to take to prevent it. Samel. Niles observd, "To What purpose do we build Schoolhouse, Set up preaching, And lay ourselves out for Public Benefit *here*, When All Our Lands are like to be Sold under us, and We turnd off, we dont know Where?"—or to that effect.

I told them that the Method devisd for their Help, in present Difficulty, was To give the Commissioners a true Account of the principal Steps, already taken, in their *Religious* and *Civil* or *Secular* Affairs, Send the Same to the Commissioners, desiring *them* to come in to their Assistance. And that *Toby Shattock*, whom I *Saw last Week*, Desird *the Heads* of the *Tribe* to meet him at *Moheague*, Any Day which *they* Should Appoint, to Consult Further on the Premises; And that I would Meet them *there*. Accordingly Appointed next Monday, 6th *July* for *that* purpose . . . .

MONDAY JULY 6. I went to Moheagen, as above appointed—Met the above Indians—Discoursed largely. Wrote Three large Letters, Two to Sr. Wm. Johnson, and one to the Commissioners.[1] Had them to Transcribe. Took me full two Days . . . .

---

[1] In his July 7, 1767, letter to Johnson, Fish gave a brief account of the history of the school and mission and noted how the Sachem's injurious practices were undermining Indian morale: "But the hopeful

prospect of *learning* and *religion* flourishing among that people has been much belated and the progress of both obstructed of late months by the unhappy disputes...which...have prevailed and greatly increased among them on account of their Sachem's selling their lands" (Arnold 1896: 46).

Honle. Andw. Olivr. Esqr.

Stoningtn. July 7. 1767.

....

At your Direction I am more particularly concerned with and for the Narraganset Tribe at Charlestown, Rhode Island. And *these* find Some Uncomfortable things, which, if not removd, threaten the Loss of all your pious Care for that poor people, viz: Their Sachems persisting, (as the Indians tell me,) in his former extravagances, especially of *Drinking* So excessively with his Companions, that his Debts, contracted thereby, are not to be dischargd but by going on to Sell their Lands, against all the Remonstrances they can make: So far as to raise a general Concern in the Tribe, lest they Should be wholly rooted out, and obligd to betake themselves elsewhere for a Living. *This* hath a very Sensible, unhappy Influence upon their religious Affairs, tending to Slacken their Attendance upon the Means of their Spiritual edification, as well as to discourage them About finishing their School house, or using Any further endeavours to establish a School Among them. To What purpose, Say they are all these pains, while our Lands are Slipping from Under our Feet, and our School House and Lott, (which, in our present Situation, we cannot Secure,) May, for ought we know, be Sold by our Sachem? Some Years Ago, The Tribe made Application to the General

Assembly of that Coloney: who So far Attended to their Complaint, as to pass Several Votes in their Favour—But nothing *done*, that hath provd effectual to redress their Grievances. Their greatest hope and Expectation, is now from General Johnson, who has heretofore wrote their Sachem, to desist that practice, of Selling Land, contrary to the Inclination of the Tribe, a Conduct, Says he, "quite repugnant to his Majesties royal Intentions, Signified by his Instructions and other ways—A Copy of which Letter, at the Indians desire, Accompanys this.[1]

I hope Sir, it will not be lookd upon by the Honourable Board, as quite out of my Province, to make this Representation, Since these Disturbances look with Such a threatning Affect upon their Spiritual and greatest Intrest; And Since it is earnestly requested of Me, by Said Indians, That, as I wish them Well, and would prove my Self their true Friend, I would Spread their Case before you, and crave your help, if any way may be devisd to Save them from this impending ruin. They very particularly desire, that your Honourable Board, if they in their Wisdom think fit, will Sollicit Sr. *William* to interpose for their Relief. A Request, of this Date, is now in readiness to be Sent to him, by a Number of Said Indians, in behalf of their Brethren But Should your Honourable Board patronize their Cause and Second their Request, it would greatly Strengthen their Hope—To which the Honourable *Com-missioners* will think it a motive, that these Indians have declined the Offer and Motion of Revd. *Mr. Greaves*, (as heretofore advisd,) choosing to Continue under the Inspection and Patronage of your Honourable Board, *They preserving their Liberty*; *in All Respects, Wherein a Free People may hope to be indulgd*. They also desire me to mention it, as an Argument in Favour of this Request, that the Narraganset Indians have ever been ready to Assist the English in all Our Wars, in which Many of their Brethren and Sons have lost their lives. I have to add, that, (as the Indians inform me,) there are *above Two hundred* of them Aggrieved, (which is more than Two Thirds of the Whole Tribe, according to their Manner, of numbring both *Sexes* and all *Ages*,) And the Number is daily increasing. Also, that as the Indians have writ to *Sr. William*, they earnestly desire that, in Case the Honourable Commissioners See fit to Sollicit him, in their Behalf, it might be done as soon as possible, that Sr. William may have it before he Acts upon *Theirs.* I presume not to dictate but Shall rest Satisfyd in the Intimations of your pleasure in the Whole Affair: but yet, Should the Commissioners do anything in Behalf of Said Indians, 'twould be taken as a Singular Favour, if their *Resolves* might be forwarded to Us with all convenient Speed, if not too great an Indulgence.

I am Sr. yr. most Obedt. humle. Servt.

JOSEPH FISH

July 17. 1767. N.B. The Within was Sent to Boston, by a Safe hand, the 13th Instant . . . .

YRS. J. FISH

[Inserted inverted in left margin:] Copy
[Inserted inverted after postscript:] For The Revd. Mr. Eleazr. Wheelock, To be Communicated To Toby Shattock[2]

Manuscript copy in the Dartmouth College Library. Another copy may be found in the Manuscript Collections of the Massachusetts Historical Society.

1 On December 1, 1764, Tobias Shattock and one other Narragansett carried a series of documents that had been prepared by their lawyer, Matthew Robinson, to William Johnson in New York. In his introduc-

tory letter Robinson wrote that "some of our Naraganset Tribe of Indians...being by far the most sensible part...have applied for several Years, to no purpose, to their Sachim...the Delays, and continuances at our General Assembly, give *Tom*, and his White Allies, and friends, much time to Serve themselves, and get good Estates from *Tom*—and the poor Tribe to be Ruined" (Hamilton and Corey 1953, XI: 405).

Johnson subsequently wrote Ninigret (in a letter since lost) to advise that the Indians should settle the dispute amongst themselves and in event they couldn't, that he would come there to help (Ibid. 483, 642). In February, 1765, the Rhode Island Assembly rejected the petition by Ephraim Coheys and Samuel Niles to restrain the Sachem, and the following month Tobias Shattock and Thomas Coheys visited Johnson again with more documents regarding their worsening case. Robinson stressed in the letter dated March 20, 1765, how difficult it would be for the Narragansett to obtain justice through the Rhode Island Assembly because members of that body as well as other influential persons were among the Sachem's main creditors (Ibid. 640-43). In a reply to Robinson, since lost, Johnson apparently offered to write to "his Majesty or Ministry" regarding the merits of the Narragansett case (Flick 1927, V: 491). Although Johnson repeated this offer in a letter to Wheelock, no record indicates that he ever followed through with it(Ibid. 683). Sachem Ninigret wrote Johnson on March 20, 1765, to explain his side of the controversy and noted that: "Wherefore as I sue, and am Sued at Common Law, Lease out my Lands in my own Right, and name which are Taxed for the Support of Government...and in all Respects obliged to Conform to the Common Law of the Realm, I therefore conceive my Situation to be very different from those Savages, and uncivilized People, over whom his Majesty has authorized you to Superintend" (Hamilton and Corey 1953, XI: 639). Ninigret's letter seems to have influenced Johnson for he informed Robinson on February 4, 1767, that the Narragansett "are a people subordinate to the laws and on a very different footing from the rest of the Indians" and therefore outside his proper authority (Arnold 1896: 56). Johnson was wary of the extent to which Rhode Island landowners would be affected by a decision in favor of Niles's group and because the opposing parties seemed to be about evenly divided, he doubted that the King's government would even take the case into consideration. Robinson, nevertheless, pleaded that "there is no hope of Redress for these poor people...Our General Assembly will not, dare not, do any thing," and that because the Sachem was now in greater debt as a result of divorce, the Indians could "really expect Ruin unless your Interposition should save them" (Flick 1927, V: 491). Still hopeful that Johnson would appeal to the King in their behalf, and perhaps unaware of his reluctance to get further involved, Niles and Shattock wrote again on February 21, 1767, to inform him that "all the land joining to the sea is already sold, that we can't in no one place go to the salt water without passing through land now in possession of the English, and that upon the smallest affront we may expect nothing better than to be prosecuted and ... deprived of the privilege of fishing, which is the main branch of support of the greatest part of our Tribe" and to express their fear that poverty would cause them and their children "to come into bondage to the English" lest Johnson do something for their relief (Arnold 1896: 30; see also Flick 1927, V: 497-98). In the letter to Johnson, which Fish wrote for Niles and Shattock on July 7, 1767, they again requested "that Your Excellency would be pleased as soon as possible to avail yourself of some method or form that may be most likely to prove effectual in intricating us out of our present distressing difficulties, to save us from beggary and destitution" (Arnold 1896: 32). Johnson did not respond to these appeals and seems to have inclined to the side of the Sachem (Stone 1865, II: 287n).

2 On April 23, 1767, Wheelock wrote a strong letter to Johnson in behalf of Tobias Shattock and the Narragansett regarding their land claims. In this letter he describes Shattock as "a Very honest, Steady, prudent Man, perhaps as much so as any of that Tribe, he is One of their Council, And I Suppose has More Influence Among them than any Other of them" (Hamilton and Corey 1957, XII: 299-300). This was not the first time that Wheelock and Johnson had corresponded over the Narragansett issue (Arnold 1896: 43-44; Hamilton and Corey 1953, XI: 961-62; O'Callaghan 1851, IV: 228).

Wheelock again wrote Johnson on August 19, 1767, to endorse Fish's July 7 statement of the Narragansett case: "Revd. Mr. Fish is, so far as I know, universally esteem'd, a gentleman of Integrity and good Ability. And accordingly the Representation he has made of the Case of the poor suffering Indians at Narraganset, is to be relied upon, as being faithfully and impartially done" (Hamilton and Corey 1957, XII: 349). In that same letter Wheelock described the Narragansett as having "bid the fairest to be built up, and became a people, of any party of Indians I know of in New England— and now just as they have got well engaged in cultivating their Lands, and begin to know the worth of them ... their best farms are slipping from under them, one after another" (Ibid. 350). Johnson replied: "I am induced to think they are much injured, and on that account I shall recommend their Case to his Majestys Ministers" (Flick 1927, V: 683).

JULY 27 ... Found the School but Small. Mr. Deake complaind, that Indians are not So Spirited as heretofore, in Sending their Children, nor equal to his seasonable Expectations, etc.

Saw Danger of the Indians being disaffected toward Me, on Account of my Late printed Sermons upon the Subject of Seperations, For which reason I discoursd largely with a Number of Indians (Some of the Heads,) before Lecture, And gave them a good deal of Satisfaction, to Appearance— Hopefully prepard their Minds for a more full Account and Light of the *Matter* and *Design* of those *Sermons*.[1] After Lecture renewd the Discourse, on the Same Subject: and believe I gave them further Satisfaction. Among other things, I told them, that doubtless *they* had run into Some Mistakes, and had got Some *false Religion*. And if So they Should be thankfull, if I had, in those Sermons, Shown them their Mistakes, which they assented to. Spent the rest of the Day in Visiting the Indians. Discoursd With Some, but most of them from Home ....

[1] This refers to *The Church of Christ* ... published in New London, 1767.

AUG. 25 ... Was prevented going Yesterday to Narraganset, by the Funeral of Widw. *Sarah Brown*, (Which I was obligd to attend,) At Which I preachd to a Large number of People; And by this Means missd An Opportunity of preaching to 200 People, Indians, Negro's and White people, Who gatherd to hear me Yesterday, at John *Shattocks*, as the Indians tell me.[1] I dont know the Meaning of this providence, but pray that God would bring good out of this (Seeming) Evil, in disappointing So Many, and giving Uneasiness to Some.

Found Indian Affairs, School etc. much as in months

Past; only Mr. Deake interrupted and much Exercisd, by An Unhappy Dispute with Wm. *Welch* who had entred a Complaint against him and Mr. Kinnion, for a most horrid Crime, of Robbing him;[2] which As Mr. Deake Says, And all others I perceive, believe, is without the least Ground or Occasion. Indians had but a few hours Notice, yet 34 Came, And Seriously Attended . . . .

1 This unexpected audience may have been in the area for the August Meeting or Powwow—an intertribal gathering for dancing, feasting, and games—held annually for about a week beginning the second Sunday in August near the church. The August Meeting may be descended historically from the pre-European harvest ritual which also was held in August (Boissevain 1975: 78-89; Simmons 1976: 226-28; Tucker 1877:65).

2 Kinnion, or Kenyon, was a common English surname in Charlestown and Westerly at this time.

OCTR. 14. 1767 . . . Preachd at John Shattocks, To about 40 (Some of them went off before Service was quite over,) So that Mr. Deake, numbring them afterwards, counted 36.

Finding that but Very few Children Attended the School Steadily, not above 12 or 13 at most Since I was here last; and nothing more done, lately, towards Finishing the School house, I thought fit, After Lecture, To Expostulate with the Indians About their Sad Neglect. Exhorted and Stirrd them up to Send their Children to School, and no longer despise So Great an Advantage, as now in their hands, to teach their Children. Told them, if they woud Shew themselves Spirited in Sending their Children, (in Case the Want of *Shoes* was one Occasion of their Neglect,) I woud give *one* or *two* pair Shoes to the most Needy. And that, if you woud go on Speedily, to finish the House, I would pay a Carpenter 2 Days, or a Common Labourer 3 Days, i.e. Give one Dollar. They Seemd to take my Exhortation in good part.

Fourth Book of Accounts of Narraganset Indian Affairs.

Journeys and Lectures to the Indians at Charlestown Rhode Island, begun June 20. 1768

....

JUNE 20. 1768 . . . . Found the School kept us as Usual, and more Schollars, of late, attending: about 15 Children, pretty Steadily come to School. Nothing Materially differing in Indians Circumstances Since last there: but Mr. Deake's Situation very difficult and distressing, on Account of his Debts. Tells me he Owes about £20- £Money, and all of it, to divers persons, now due, by Notes of hand or Obligations on Demand. His Creditors Patience no longer to be expected. Two Notes already committed to hands of Authority, to be heard. He expects a *Writ* or Two, before this Week is out: And can't See Any Way to avoid being taken out of his Business; which must break up the School. The Consequence he Apprehends will be, That the Indians, From their great Regard to Mr. *Greaves* N. Londo., Will Make Application to *Him,* or to the *Church* of England for a Schoolmaster and *Support.* On Consulting his Case, I promised him to write the Commissioners in his Behalf.

A[t] about Two, Preachd at Indian Meeting house, to 20 Indians, (They having heard that I would not Come today, and Numbers of them, through Carelessness, having forgot the Lecture.) From Matth: 22.39. *Thou Shalt love thy*

42

Neighbour as Thy Self—A grace and Duty much Wanting and greatly Neglected Among these Indians. In the Fore part of My Discourse, Indians Seemd Sleepy and Careless—Digressed and rousd them, by Awakening Touches. Towards the Close of my Discourse, A Molatto (Ammon,) a Lusty Man, having for Some time discoverd Something Singular in his Countenance, fell into great distress, manifested by Crying out bitterly, which continued through the Remainder of Sermon. Finishd off with a fervent Prayer, trembling as he Spoke. Found upon Speaking to him after Sermon, that the Word reachd his Conscience, Wakd up a Sense of his Guilt, in late evil Conduct, having been long reputd a Christian, but of late Years or Months, walkd unbecoming his Profession. Several other Indians, manifested Some deep Impressions from the *Word*.

After Lecture, Visited Two Families. Wm. Sachem (of the Sachems Party and his Uncle,) who never heard me preach Save once. Found him Serious and Attentive, while I talkd to him on the Affairs of his Soul. Has got a hope of Grace, in Former times but for Years past lives poorly. I endeavourd to Awake him to a Sense of his Duty and Danger. Here found about a Dozen Indians, Men and Women, who had been *Hoeing* for Will. I gave *Them* an Exhortation, and proceeded to find *Toby*.

The Indians commonly Fence their Fields with thick *Hedges*—No *Barrs*, I was obligd to break through their Hedges, with my Horse, and repair them, Well as I could. After travelling through the Thickets, many times no path, and passing deep valleys and Steep Hills, over Which I could but just climb, with my Horse in hand, for near 3/4 hour, (Mr. Deake in company my Guide) I found Sqr. *Tobys* (as Calld,) living much retird and then Alone. He's the Oldest Indian Man, in the Tribe. In his 86th Year.[1] Entirely (or Near it) *blind*. Reckoned (not without good reason,) a pious Man. Talkd familiarly of *Death* and *Heaven*. Said he longd to go Home to his Fathers house, which he hopd for, in a little time. Twas now Night. Took leave of the Old Man . . . .

1 Probably Toby Coyhes (see diary, March 27, 1769). If this was the Toby Cohoise, said by Stiles in 1761 to be "the oldest Indian alive, and who remembers K. Philip's War and the Swamp Fight, A.D. 1675," he would have been considerably older than eighty-six (Dexter 1916: 115).

TUESDAY, JUNE 21. Returnd to the Indian houses, in the Morning. Visitted Four Indian Families. Discoursed with a Christian Indian Woman, (*Henry Harrys* Wife,) Under Soul Trouble, declining Health and many Afflictions. Her Daughter (a Widow) A bed with a Bastard Child—I endeavourd to awake the poor thoughtless, unconcernd Creature to a Sense of her Guilt and Danger. Calld at [?*Sachs*] Daughters—Droppd a Word of encouragement to a poor Creature in Travail.

Visited old Robins. His Daughter an Impudent Secure, Lewd person—Two Bastard Children with her. I endeavourd to Alarm her Conscience, by Shewing the certain Destruction of *Fornicators* etc.

Visited John *Shattock*, And, among other things, Reprovd him for not reading the *Bible* (as he Says he Can read it Well,) in his Family daily. Owns he has not read it for a long time. I endeavourd to Convince him of his Sinfull neglect, and excite him to his Duty. Left the Indians between Ten and Eleven o'Clock, and returnd home by post Road . . . .

MONDAY JULY 18. 1768 . . . Very hot and I much unwell; but reachd the School house about *One*. The School kept up, and about the Number of Schollars as before (15, or more) . Mr. Deake Somewhat relievd of the pressures mentiond in

Journal of last Visit. He approved of my Proposal to Commissioners for advancing half a years pay—Said twould much relieve him.

Many people at the Indian Meeting, Yesterday (Lords day,) English and Indians. Numbers behavd very wickedly, in time of the Indians Worship. In the day time or Evening Some of Them got drunk and Two Squaws fell upon another Squaw, that was heavy with Child, and beat, kickd and abusd her, So that her Life was much doubted of.

Preachd at Indian Meeting house to 30 Indians, Chiefly Women and young persons, from Matth. 5.4. Nothing Special Appeard in the Audience.

After Lecture Visited Samel. *Niles*, (about 1½ Mile North East from Meeting house) intending, to have Spent the Remainder of the Day and Next Day Forenoon, in Visiting Indians: but Mr. Deake and Niles told me there was (likely,) Scarce An Indian to be found at home; As the Busy Season calld them Abroad. So thought it pity to Spend my time, in Visiting Empty Houses. Concluded to deferr my intended Visits to the Next Journey.

....

MONDAY AUGT. 15. 1768 . . . Mr. Deake in his School—but 6 or 8 Schollars, for a Week or Fortnight past and even now. Indians Shamefully Negligent of their great Privilege—Parents no Government of their Children, in *Obliging* them to go to School. Tis hard to know What will engage them to be Steady!

The *School-House* Still neglected—No motion towards finishing of it. Consulted with Mr. Deake what measures are next to be taken, to Compleat the Work. Concluded on a method, as below.

Preachd, at the Meeting house, to 33 Indians, from Jno. 3.14.15. *As Moses lifted up the Serpent, in the Wilderness etc.* Introducd the Discourse, by a narrative of Israelites travelling through the Wilderness, And, for their Murmuring Against God and Moses, bitten by Firy Serpents. Read and Explaind the 21st Chapter of Numbers, which gives Account of the brazen Serpent and the Cause of its being Made, Set up, etc. to help their Understanding of our Saviours Discourse, in the Text. Had a Serious and Attentive Auditory.

Immediately After the Blessing, gave the Indians a Solemn Warning and Exhortation, upon that awfull Event of the *Indian Womans* Death, (Spoken of July 18, who died of her wounds that day, for which *one* Squaw was Apprehended, and Committed to Prison,) Admonishing of them, that their Sinfull, Shamefull Neglect and Contempt of their precious Privileges, in not Sending their Children to Learn nor better Attending the preaching of the Gospel, at Lectures etc. was So offensive to God, Who had Shown them Such great Favours, that he was hereby justly provoked to leave them to their own hearts Lusts, (Drunkenness, whordom, malice and Revenge,) which Occasiond the Death of *that* Miserable, wicked Woman, Then big with her Fourth bastard *Child.* . . . The Serious Indians, very thankfull for the Plain, and Justly Severe, Rebuke.

After Lecture and public Exhortation, Visited John Shaddick and Family, under Sore Affliction, on the (probable,) Death of their *Two* Sons in England; *Supposed,* by public prints, to have Died 9th of May last in Edingburgh, with the Small Pox, (i.e. *One* Said to be dead *then,* and the other in a bad way) .[1] Left *Johns* at Sunset, And Lodged at Collo. Champlins.[2]

[1] Following receipt of Fish's July 7, 1767, letter, Andrew Oliver wrote the Rhode Island Assembly regarding the deed to the schoolhouse lot and the assembly temporarily restrained Ninigret from further disposing of reservation property (Bartlett 1861, VI: 529-30; McCallum 1932: 206-7). In October, 1767, however, the assembly resolved

that a committee be appointed to determine the extent of Ninigret's debts and to "dispose of so much of the Indian lands, as may be sufficient to discharge the just debts" (Bartlett 1861, VI: 533). Tobias Shattock wrote Wheelock that this decision would ruin the tribe, and that he would sail to England to seek redress from the Earl of Dartmouth and the King (McCallum 1932: 208). Niles and five other members of their council wrote Wheelock also to explain that they were "in tribulation on account of our lands, being disposed of contrary to our minds" and apologized for keeping Tobias and John Shattock from their studies, "as we have none so capable of doing business as they are, we are obliged to" (McClure and Parish 1811: 277). Tobias informed the Rhode Island Assembly that "their last Resolve on Indian affairs, in my sincere Opinion is Grievous. . . . I've tho't certain Gentlemen has endeavoured to advance their Interest by the poor Indians, thinking (perhaps) their extream Poverty, may prevent their being called into Question" (Kimball 1903, II: 399). Ever hopeful that Johnson would act decisively in their behalf, and with encouragement from Wheelock and Graves, both John and Tobias left together for England in winter, 1768 (Flick 1928, VI: 80-82, 87-89; McCallum 1932: 206-10). On May 6, 1768, shortly after their arrival, Tobias died of smallpox in Edinburgh. Their host in Edinburgh, Alexander Mowbray, wrote Wheelock that "the Soul took wing a quarter before 4 on Friday Morning the 6th instant . . . the best people in Town were Invitted and attended the Funeral and in our Church yard [Grayfriars] was interred the first Christian Indian that ever we heard of" (McCallum 1932: 213). John recovered and continued on to London but was completely unsuccessful and returned to America in September (Love 1899: 72-74; McCallum 1932: 208-14). The October, 1767, decision by the Rhode Island Assembly to sell more Indian land to repay Ninigret's debts and the failure of the Shattocks' mission were sorely disheartening to the Narragansett plaintiffs, most of whom thereafter lost interest in Fish's preaching and in sending their children to Deake's school.

2 Christopher Champlin was a prominent Charlestown planter, an Anglican, and a veteran of the French and Indian War. Col. Champlin, who was a close associate of Ninigret, kept the Sachem's credit records and acquired much of his land (Arnold 1896: 47-48; Arnold 1860, II: 191, 198; Champlin Papers 1751-57; Denison 1878: 156; Weeden 1910: 148).

TUESDAY AU[G]T. 16. 1768. Returned Seasonably, this Morning, to Indian *Town*, And Went up as far as to Samel. Niles's, About 5 or 6 Miles, from the Collo[ne]ls. Calld

Again at Jno. Shaddicks, (absent last Night,) now at home—Discoursd largely with him and Family, on the Subject of their (Supposed) *Sons Death*—Gave them the best Instructions, Directions and Cautions, I could; which Seemd to be Very Acceptable. They all behavd Decently, Shewing a Christian becoming Temper. Talkd also, a few words, with Jno. About the *Glass*, Nails, etc. Books etc. Given by the Commissioners for the house and School, which were Under his Care. Excusd *Him*, for the present, from concerning himself, much, about finishing the House: but Said he would Lend a hand etc.

Calld at Mr. *Deake's*, and talkd further About the *House* etc. Concluded to Engage *James Daniel* and Samel. Niles, to Compleat the Work. Went to *James Daniels* and proposd the matter to him, who freely Consented to Undertake it, if *Sam Niles* woud join him. Went to *Sam Niles's*, who readily complyd to Join *James Daniel*—Returnd to *James Daniels*, And told him of *Niles's* freedom to engage etc. Left the Affair Wholly with *them Two* (not excluding John *Shaddick*, in what he woud freely do,) And *They* engagd to take the Whole Business upon themselves—to find all the Boards and Clapboards, and to take the Commissioners pay. Are to enter upon the Work Soon as necessary Business admits—to draw in What Indian Help they can, and hope to go through and finish the House this Fall. *These Two* being the most able, forehanded and thorough Men (among all the Indians) And Well agreed to Carry on Business together (though *Daniel* is of the *Sachems* party, but a moderate, honest good man), I am now in greater hopes, than ever, of Seeing the House finishd (except plaistering) this Fall . . . .

MONDAY, SEPTR. 12. 1768 . . . Found the School (for ought I could See,) Well Attended—18 Schollars. Had the News of *Toby Shattocks* Death Confirmd—he died, of the Small Pox, in Edingborough the 6th of May last, (but his Brother Jno. is recoverd). Saw and Conversd with his Father, Mother and Widow. All behavd decently, and receivd an Exhortation Well. Nothing further Special Among the Indians, Since last here.

About Two o'Clock, Preachd, at the Meeting house from Pm.93.5—*Holiness becometh thine house etc.* To 46 Indians, Most of them Men and Women. Gave Serious Attention, except 4. or 5. (Young Indians—Lads,) went out of Meeting, Midst of Service; N.B. heard *Since*, they were on a Days Work, and could not Stay longer. After I had finishd, Jno. Shattock gave his Testimony to the Truths Saying, (though through his Weakness,) that he had nothing to Say, for Every thing had been Said. I admonishd them For that ill Custom, of going out of Meeting (and Sometimes not returning) in time of Service—Reprovd and Exhorted Parents to Advise their Children better and Restrain them, if they Could. Told the young people, that as to *Man* it was ill *Manners*; And as to God, a Contempt of his Word, and So offensive to him . . . .

TUESDAY SEPR. 13. Returnd to the Indians. Met Mr. Deake at James Niles's—He went with me to Conduct me to a little Neighbourhood, 2 or 3 Miles South East from Meeting House. I Went to Seven *Wigwams*—Two of the Families Absent, The Rest, at least Some of them, at home.

But *Two* persons, of these Five Families (i.e. of them that I discoursd with,) that come to Lectures, and these have heard me but once. They Objected nothing Against *me* or my preaching, but Said (Some of them) the reason of their not Coming to Lecture was, old Quarrels and Contentions *with* and among their Brethren. Suggested that Some of the Indians would not like to See them at Lecture, neither did

they want to See them. I endeavourd to Shew them the Evil
of Such a Spirit and Way—Exhorted them to Forgiveness,
Unity etc. and to Attend the Preaching of Gospel, for their
Own Souls good, as they would not be found Guilty of Casting Contempt upon Christ and his offerd Salvation, etc. etc.
Addressd my Self particularly to Each One in their Turns,
and they gave a Serious Attention. One of them An Indian
Woman, Mother of Children, told me, She never [. . .] had
any Conviction of her Lost Estate, her need of Christ, etc.,
nor ever had any *concern* about her Soul etc. Was one of
the most remarkable Instances of total Security and Insensibility that I ever met with!

Eat Victuals at one of the Wigwams And About *One* or
Two Shaped my Course from the *Woods* to the *Post Rhode*
(*that* way most Convenient from this part of the Indian Set-
tlements, for home,) reachd Collo. Champlins about Two
or Three (16 Miles from home,) and after Refreshing my
Self and horse, proceeded on my Journey, And reachd home
in the Evening . . . .

MONDAY OCTOBR. 10. 1768 . . . Preachd at the Indian Meeting house, to 24 Indians, from Gal: 3.14. *That We might
receive the Promise of the Spirit through Faith.* Indians
Seem to Set but little Store by the Lectures—a very dull
time—have reason to lament my own Barrenness and Unsuccessfullness. Numbers, near the Meeting house, about
their Own work: And Some, I Suppose, hindred, too easily,
by their entring this day, on the Business of finishing the
Schoolhouse. This is the Third Lecture Successively, that
Sam Niles has been Absent; Though (when I askd him,
After the Lecture, as he Came in my way) he would not
own that he was Absent on Account of any Objection
Against me; but as he had been much Abroad of late, he
could not Attend as usual.

After Lecture, Spent the Remainder of the Day with Mr. Deake, Samel. Niles and others, in Viewing the School house, Enquiring about Boards, Stuff and Materials to carry on and finish the Building. Orderd the Front *Wall* to be taken down, and better Plank put up before the Clapboards were naild on, As the Wall was put up of Very thin, poor *boards* instead of Planks. A Teem and Several hands, now at work digging and Drawing Stones for the *Hearths*. Orderd the Work to be Carried on With Expedition. Drew An Order upon Mr. *Pease* of N. Port, to Let the Indians have 2500, 8 dny. Nails and 1000, 10 dy.[1] Ditto for the School House. And, wrote him that his Account Should be draw at for (by me,) on the Commissioners Boston. The School must Stop, While at work on the House. Mr. Deake is going to Doctr. Wheelocks. Set out after Sunset—rode in the Night to Capt. Wells's . . . .[2]

[1] Eight-penny and ten-penny nails.
[2] Probably Captain Edward Wells, Jr., a soldier, merchant, and deputy to the Rhode Island Assembly, from Hopkinton (Bartlett 1861, VI: 144, 177, 321, 523).

MONDAY NOVR. 7. 1768 . . . After Discoursing with Mr. Deake about affairs of the School, Indians etc. preachd, at the School house, from Rom: 8.13. *For if ye live After the Flesh, ye Shall die: but if ye through the Spirit mortifie etc.* Found my Self in a very low Frame—Empty, Dry and barren. Was enabled, I trust, to Speak the Truth, indeed, but had So little of a feeling Sense of what I deliverd, that I was even Ashamd and much discouragd. And what made me Still more heartless, but Twelve Indians old and Young to hear me. Looks as if my Mission *here* was drawing to a Close. Lord humble and Quicken me.

Mr. Deake begins his School again to Morrow: having

Omitted it ever Since I was here before, on Account of the Indians being At Work on the School house.

The House almost finishd, except plaistering. But Three or four at Work. They tell me, that in 2 or 3 days more they hope to finish Clapboarding, The Pitch on etc. but must Stop, for the present, on Account of their own Business. The Indians, in General, have droppd all their Spirit for this public Work.

Drew an Order on Esqr. Oliver, in Favour of Mr. Pease, for Sh 27/. £Money, for Nails for the House, which Mr. Pease helpd them to; viz: 2500, 8 dny. 1000, 10 dny. Wrote a Letter to Esqr. Oliver, informing the Occasion of wanting So many mo[re] Nails, viz: The Carpenters Mistake etc. Spent the Evening with Jno. *Shaddock* at house, with a View to Compose a Difference between him and the Church, the Church having Cut him off, or Cast him out, for Some offence.[1]

Jno. Shaddock Informd Me, that Mr. Baccus's Books Against me Were plenty among them, And, Supposd, that was one Reason Why So few Attended the Lecture.[2]

Hear that Sam Niles Said, he did not want me to preach to them; And Attended my Lectures, only because I befriended them About their School.

I lay this Intelligence up, and Shall watch for the Issue . . . .

---

[1] Samuel Drake's account from this period may explain why John Shattock was expelled from the church: "if, at any time, any of their brethren return to their former sinful practices, the rest will mourn over them as though their hearts would break: that, if their backsliding brethren repent of their sin, and manifest a desire to walk again with the church, their rejoicing is equal to their former mourning: but . . . if no fruit of repentance appears, after they have mourned over them for several meetings, they bid the offender farewel, as though they were going to part to meet no more, and with such a mourning as resembles a funeral" (Beatty 1768: 107-8).

2 Isaac Backus (1724-1806), a prominent New England Separate Baptist clergyman and writer, published in 1768 a rebuttal to Fish's nine sermons on the separations in his North Stonington congregation. In this book, entitled *A Fish caught in his own Net. An Examination of Nine Sermons, from Matt. 16.18. Published last year, by Mr. Joseph Fish of Stonington* . . . ,Backus defended the doctrine of the internal call and documented the unfair treatment of Separates in Massachusetts and Connecticut. Backus also had mentioned Fish in two previous publications, *The Internal Call* . . . (1754), and *A Letter to the Reverend Mr. Benjamin Lord* . . . (1764), and when Fish replied in 1771 with *The Examiner Examined* . . . , Backus wrote *An Address to Joseph Fish* . . . , which was published in 1773 (McLoughlin 1967; 1968: 168-70).

Fifth Book 1769
Account of Indian Affairs—Narraganset

....

JANY. 2d. . . . Preachd to 23. Indians and Some White people from Ezekel. 33.11. *Turn ye turn ye* etc. Indians Seemd to Set patiently to hear plain Dealing.

The House, nigh finishd. One Days work of 2 or 3 hands, will finish the outside. The Windows up—Glass fixd in, but not puttied.

The School kept: but not Many Schollars yet. Mr. Deake Unwell. Found Mr. Deake had done So much and engagd the rest, i.e. to pay, I judgd that he deservd the Five Dollars, given by the Commissioners. And So I paid him Three Dollars, which with the Two I paid them of my own Money, when here last, Makes the Five. Seeing Mr. Deake in a very poor afflicted Situation—hard Service, at backing all his Wood, and hard Fare—In a low State of Health, but a little Provision, and Mrs. Deake, (a worthy good woman,) near her Time etc. I gave him half a Dollar. And on my Return at Doctr. Babcocks, Thinking I had not done enough, I bought and Sent him ½lb. Tea and 2lb. Sugar.[1]

Settled Accounts with the Indians, And paid Sam Niles and James Daniel, and took their Receipt for £8.00.3 . . . .

[1] Joshua Babcock (1707-83), who lived in a large house still standing on the Post Road in Westerly, was a Yale graduate and a prominent physician, merchant, and farmer, in addition to being a Justice in the Rhode Island Supreme Court and Westerly representative in the General Assembly for about forty years. He also was one of the first corporators of Brown University and a major general of the Rhode Island

Militia in 1776 (Arnold 1860, II: 359; Biographical Cyclopedia 1881: 113; Cole 1889: 248-49; Denison 1878: 120-22, 157-58; Weeden 1910: 295-96).

JANY. 30. 1769 . . . Found a Large School, about 30 Schollars, Some of them (at least One) Married Women, Widw. Hanh. *Shattuck*. Numbers of them Young Women grown. A hopefull Appearance of Learning Among the Youth.

The Indians Much pleasd and affected with Mr. Kinne's late Visit and preaching to them.[1] Whoever the Lord Shall honour, as An Instrument to enlighten, convince and Convert them, Will, I trust, afford Me entire Satisfaction and matter of Joy.

Preachd to 34 Indians—great and Small—from Matth: 22d. 42, by Way of Question and Answer; And Appointed them Another Lecture, This day Four Weeks, viz: 27.Feb: if Season permit.

Left Mr. Deakes after Sun Set. Visited Jno. Shattucks, his Son Jno. being Sick . . . .

[1] Aaron Kinne (1744-1824) was a Yale graduate who worked as a missionary among the Oneida of New York and for many years as a minister in Groton, Connecticut. Fish may not have thought well of Kinne whose religious views were controversial (McLoughlin 1979, II: 879n; National Cyclopaedia 1929, VI: 439; Dexter 1916: 307, 413; Weis 1936: 121).

. . . FEB: 27. 1769. Very bad Travelling and I much indisposd With a bad Cold. Did nothing at Visiting this Journey, nor did I perceive any thing Special among the Indians. Preachd at John Shadducks to Sixty Indians, Including Negros, From Matth: 22.42. Upon Christs Righteousness. Felt Somewhat Free of Speech: but had not, in my Self, that feeling Sense of the Great Truths that were deliverd, which I wishd for. The Indians were, Some of them, attentive and Affected. Others Seemd Very Careless;

as if they did not like to be taught doctrine So Well as to have there passions fird. I fear they have not Much desire to *Learn* Truth . . . .

....

MAR: 27. 1769 A Stormy Morning made me late From home, but reachd the Indians in Season. Found a Small Number met at John Shattucks. Preachd to about 15 or 20 from 1 Tim:2.5. *One Mediator* etc. Had Some what more of Sensibility of Truths delivered, than when here last. Indians Seem to grow more and More Careless About Religion. I fear their General Plight and Contempt of the Gospel and Means of Grace and Learning Will Soon deprive them of *Both*.

Revd. Mr. *Park* present and made Last Prayer, with great Seriousness and Propriety. School kept up; but a Very few Schollars. Mr. Deake under Many Discouragements—His Wife *abed* and low, Family increasing and Small Means. I proposd that would come up to Stoninght. and See if he Might meet with Any Relief.

Told the Indians I was going Journey to N. Haven, could not be here again this day *4 Weeks*: but This day 5 Weeks viz: 1 *May* would endeavour to come down And Spend *that* day in Visiting the Indians, and the next day vz: *Tuesday* May 2d 10, o'Clock, give a Lecture at the Aged *Toby Coyhes*, if he is desirous of it or Willing to receive it.

....

MAY 1. 1769 Rode down to Narraganset. Visited Mr. Deake, And found his School very Small indeed—3, 4; 5, etc., And Some days none at All. The Indian Children very Destitute of Clothing, And, *all* very Slothfull. Mrs. Deake in a Suffering Condition—Cant possibly Stand it, much longer. No Relief from the Commissioners, nor Any Return to My Letter, in his behalf.

Went Visiting to Nine Indian houses and Wigwams. Found but 4 of the heads of Families At home, So could not talk So much With them as I intended. And This is commonly the Case. They are careless About Lectures; So that I cannot instruct Many there: and Almost always gone from home. The Cause of Christ, Among them has numerous Enemies, especially from Among the English.

TUESDAY MAY 2d. About 12 o'Clock, preachd at Jno. Shattucks, to 13 Indians. Appointed the Next Lecture at the School house, on the Monday After their Next Sacraments viz: May 22d—2 o'Clock . . . .

MONDAY MAY 22 . . . Preachd at the School house, to Mr. Deakes Family and 4 Indians. It looks as if my Service among These Indians draws nigh to an end. They are all about their own Business, or taking their own Ways—Some at Labour, and others at their Diversions. A Considerable Number of Indians, at next house, in Sight of the Lecture, Making themselves Merry, with drink (I'm told,) And at their Sports. The Soberest of them, Calld, Christian Indians, (I am informd) have nourishd their Jealousys, into Realities—Are, at present, fixd in their prejudices Against me; not against my Person or Preaching—they own I preach the Truth: but will not come to hear me, chiefly, they Say, because I take Money of my Own people, for preaching; So Am a Hireling, And therefore cant be a true Minister of Jesus Christ. They Are Also taught by the Spirit, immediately from Heaven: So have teachings above the Bible. They also Suspect that I am Seeking the Dominion Over them, in Some Form or Other; And Are Afraid of Their Liberties. These, and many Such groundless Surmises Are Infusd, fomented and riveted in them (Im told,) by the Un-friendly, Ignorant, Self-Conceited, Enthusiastick *English* Among them, who are connected with them, And industri-ously Strive to break off the Indians, from My Ministry.

Consulted what was best for me to do. Was advisd and Desird, by the Few that were there, to Come again, This day 4 Weeks; And not give up the Cause, for these Dis-couragements. Which I complyd with.

. . . Mr. Deake had not One Indian Schollar today; And but few, Sometimes None, last Week. Is under great Dis-couragements. The *School* and *Lectures* are, generally, At-tended much alike.

Appointed the Next Lecture, at John Shattucks, This day 4 Weeks. There being nothing to be done at present, while Indians are in this Situation (none to [be] found at home,) I returnd the Same day, at night . . . .

. . . MONDAY JUNE 19. 1769. Mr. Deake observd, that his School and my Lectures are alike poorly attended. They Seem to keep pair with each other. He has but about 3 or 4. as Schollars. Said further, that Since the Indians have grown So cold about the Lectures and School, Wickedness Awfully Abounds Among them. They grow worse and worse apace. I visited *Sam. Niles* (Mr. Deake with me,) before Lecture. Askd him the Reason of his Leaving my Lecture, those months past. He assignd only This reason for it, viz: "My Taking Money of my people for Preaching, And his Indian Brethren Twitted him for coming to hear *one* that takes money" etc. I told how my people, at Settling, of their own accord, proposd the Terms, and of their own free Will made the Covenant. So that twas their own Choice. How-ever I am not Chargeable to the Indians. Like *Paul,* "I have robbed other Churches, Taking Wages of *them,* to do the

Indians Service—Rehearsd my Coming among them, agre-
able to their own Choice—My Labour and Service in preaching and about their School etc. That if they had any Teachings beside what was found in the Bible, twas not of God.
Left with him Pauls words, to Timo., Holy *Scriptures* which
are able to instil life etc. All Scripture is given by Inspira-
tion etc. that the Man of God may be [?present] etc. etc.

Preachd, 2 o'Clock, at Jno. Shattucks—from Canticles
2.3. to about 18 Indians. Discoursd with them freely, after
Lecture. Returnd home, Same day, per Post Road, late at
Night . . . .

. . . JULY 17. to preach Lecture to the Narraganset Indians
Charlestown. Per J. Fish. Preachd at Jno. Shattocks, to 16
Indians, From Heb: 2.3. *How Shall We escape if We Neglect So great Salvation.* Had Something of Freedom, And a
Serious Auditory, what I hope Receivd Benifit. Some Spake
in Favour of the School, which, at present, is much Neglected, As in Accounts Above. After Lecture discoursd
freely, with Indians present, About the School and Lecture.
Perceivd that tis the design and Endeavour of Satan and his
Instruments to root out both School and Lecture, that he
may Regain and hold his Kingdom Among these Indians:
but hope, by the Help of God, to frustrate his design . . . .

AUGT. 14. 1769 . . . Found the School had been increasing
Since last journey—About 10 Schollars a Day. Some hopes
that the School wont be broke up for want of Childrens
being Sent.

Preachd at the Meeting house to 17 Indians and Some
English, from Rev: 3.17.18. *Thou Sayst I am rich etc.* But
a few of their Church present. Sam Niles and most of his
brethren have left the Lecture. They endeavour to brace
up to Strengthen themselves Against Me, on Account of my

taking Salary at home; but perhaps the true reason is, They think themselves rich as having their Teachings directly from heaven. Their Church Will, and, I think, must come down; they having No Bible in their Church, nor Church Covenant, are much lost and Confusd, and cannot Stand.

I think to keep possession there as long as I can, endeavouring by preaching the Gospel there, to do what I can to destroy the kingdom of Satan, And build up Christs.

....

SEPTR. 4. 1769... School kept as Usual—From 6. and 12 Schollars, and rather on the increasing order. Preachd from Jno. 3.19.—*Light is come into the world and man loved darkness rather than Light etc.*

The Indians, I learn by Deake and Jno. Shattuck, are generally prejudicd Against All the Learned, Standing Ministers. Yesterday, *Sam Niles*, in his preachment, came out fully and plainly Against them. Said these learned Ministers Are Thieves Robbers, Pirates etc. They Steal the word. God told the Prophets the words they Spoke: and These Ministers Steal that Word. etc. etc. Is full bitter against them.

The greatest part of his Discourse, (I'm told,) was gross Error. Ignorance, Railing, outpourings of Ignorance.

I endeavourd to teach and Establish, those that heard me, in Bible Truth—Divine Revelation, as recorded in Scripture. Was Somewhat free, plain, bold in declaring Against Satans Delusions and Wiles, to draw the Indians off from adhering to the Truth, as Exhibited in the preached Gospel. Found my Self Somewhat engagd Against the *Devil* and his Instruments. Am not Discouragd—The Devil *was* Vanquishd by Christ, And by Force of *Truth*. He may be So again . . . .

Appointed Next Lecture This day 4 Weeks, viz: Octr. 2d at one o'Clock, The Monday *Before* their Sacrament.

....

OCTR. 2d. 1769... The School kept, but poorly attended, by Children—but *one* Schollar to day, and but About ½ Dozn. a Day last Week. The Indians Seem Stupidly to Neglect and Despise the Privilege.

Preachd, at the Meeting house, from 1 Pet: 4.18. *If Righteous Scarcely Saved, Where Shall the Ungodly and Sinner Appear?*

This day The Indians had a *Bush Cut*ting and Quilting Frolick, or Entertainment; which might be one Reason, Why So few (as 6. Indians) Attended the Lecture. Besides, Samel. Niles (as Mr. Deake informs me,) dos all he can to prevent the Indians coming to hear me. Yesterday he publickly declaimd Against Standing Ministers and Talks of Scripture; but makes [up] the most and Abuses the Rest ....

OCTR. 23. 1769... School as last Journey—Preached at Meeting house, to 7 Indians Luke 16.31. *If they hear* NOT *Moses and the Prophets etc.* Am Informd that Sam Niles continues his enmity Against The ministers, as usual. Speaks also against Learning. Believe he will do his own Business, i.e. by his Railing, instead of preaching the Gospel, convince the More Sensible Indians, that he has a bad Cause. I purpose to Continue preaching the Gospel to them.

....

To The Honourable Andrew Oliver Esqr. / Boston / per Cpt. Rhodes[1]

Stonington, 25th Octobr. 1769.
HONLE. ANDW. OLIVER ESQR.

Sir, ...

My *Lecture* at Narraganset has, for Some Months past, been under Frowns and Discouragements by reason of a bad Spirit that has reignd Among Many of the Indians. They have conceived a Strong prejudice against all the Learned Standing Ministers, (as I'm told,) on Account of their taking *Support* of their Own people etc. They Say also that, although We preach the *Truth*, (They Suppose,) as it is in the Bible, yet *that* is not true preaching; because we depend upon what the *Bible* Says, and not upon what the *Spirit* teaches—that *They* have their Teaching directly from the Fountain, So above *ours*. By which, and Other like Notions, the holy Scriptures are but lightly Set by, and *Learning* not much esteemd. *Sam Niles*, their Teacher, has, of late (as I'm informd,) done all he could, in public and private, to discourage the Indians from attending my *Lecture*, and, by his low opinion of Learning, eventually discourages the *School*.

I have seriously enquird what is my Duty—have taken the Same pains for their good, as usual, though have not *Visited* So much, at their houses, this Summer; it being impossible to find them at home. It has been grievous to perform Such a Journey, and go through so much Exercise, to Serve a people that, in General, Set no Store by my Labours. I have also been concernd about taking the *public Money*, when So few come to hear me of late, as the Inclosed Account Shews. And, on the Whole, Should have dropped the *Lecture*, at least for a while, had it not been for these reasons: That a number of the Indians are desirous of my continuing to preach to them; And it Seems hard to leave them, When they Stand in Such Special need of Instruction; and not right, to give up So important a Cause, at this Critical Juncture, When *Satan* is So manifestly and powerfully Striving to *regain*, or *hold* his Kingdom, (Shook by the Gospel Ministry,) among those poor Indians, by Error and Ignorance, as the above discovers. By the *Lectures*, I trust, a Measure of *divine Truth* is dealt out to a *number*, which may Serve to Restrain the Enemy, preserve the place from total Apostacy, and finally prove as a Grain of *Mustard Seed*. Besides, I'm inclined to think, that Satans Rage, by *Sam's* bitter Railing at us, and thereby discouraging *Lectures* and *School* together, Will, e're long, convince the more Sensible and Serious Indians, that the Opposition is from *their* Enemys quarter; and that *Sam* is doing them the greatest Mischief by discouraging Lectures and Learning. So, Conclude to continue my Service to those Indians as usual, if not advisd, per honourable Commissioners, to desist.

There were Some Special Reasons for the Two last Lectures being So thin, (a public Entertainment by One of the Indians etc.) which hope wont take place for the future.

One or two of my Lectures were Appointed Short of a month, by reason of my being Obligd to take long Journeys. For the like reason, Shall be obligd, at other times, to exceed a month: So dont mean to multiply Lectures beyound Order. Should not have drawn So soon, were it not that I dont expect Any Other Opportunity this Fall, (not thinking to come down my Self,) and could not See how to defer it till Spring. With Sincere, dutifull Regards to Hon[le.] Commissrs., Am, Hond. Sir, your Very humle. Servt.

JOSEPH FISH

Stonington Decr. 4. 1769—

SIR,

I break open my Letter to Observe, That, failing of the Conveyance, which I thought was certain, when I wrote the Above, I have Visited the *Narragansets* once Since, And had more Encouragement than at Some Lectures before—Some hopefull Tokens of the Divine Presence—More Hearers—An Invitation from a Principal Indian, of the *Sachems* Party, to preach the next Lecture at his House etc.—As also to draw my Account New, and prepare Orders by Another Hand.

Fish papers in the Manuscript Collections of the Connecticut Historical Society.

[1] Captain Simon Rhodes (1716-84) was born in Newport, R.I., but moved to Stonington where he purchased large tracts of land (Wheeler 1900: 554).

[*Easter Sermon Outline*]

Apr. 16. 1770. At [. . .], Narraganset. And at our Indian Town [. . .] Monday before.

Mark 16.15.16. Go ye into all the world and preach the Gospel to Every Creature. He that believeth and is baptized Shall be Saved: but he that believeth not Shall be damned.

Explain the word, Shewing what is meant by Gospel—Good Saying—glad tidings—News of a Saviour—and all the Lasting Truths of Scripture, *de illo*. [?Where] to preach it—publish, declare etc. Every Creature—All rational Creatures—All Nations, as Matthew.

He that Believeth—Receiveth Christ, giveth full Credit to his Truths, evidencd by hearty obedience. And if Baptized—

with water in the Name etc. Shall be Saved—from Sin,—an Eternal Salvation.

Believeth not Damned—Sent to hell to dwell with Devils, to all eternity.

That you may See the Weight and Importance of this Scripture, and take it to heart, I'll endeavour [I].D. to Shew.

1. The State—The Miserable State and Condition that all Men Are in by Nature; And how they come into Such a State.

2. The Absolute need they Stood in of a Saviour, to answer for them and to deliver them. Man without Strength.

3. Who the Saviour is: or what Manner of Person he must be—J. Cht., Son of God, Son of Man.

4. The care that God took to make the Saviour known to Man, from the beginning. To Adam and Eve, our First Father and Mother.

Gen: 3.15.	*The Seed of the Woman etc.* known to the Ancients to be Christ the Saviour.
Gen: 23.18.	In Thy Seed All Nations Earth blessed.
Gal: 3.v.16.	Till the Seed Should come to whom promise made.
	And to thy Seed, which is Christ.
	And hence Said
Gal: 3.8.	*The Gospel was preached to Abraham.* He knew Christ the Saviour—Saw him by Faith.
	Moses Spoke of Christ
Deut: 18.15.	A prophet Ld. your God. raise up etc. Applyd to Christ
Acts 3.22.	Moses truely Said etc. A *Prophet* etc.
Isaiah 7.14.	A *Virgin* Shall conceive and bear a Son.
Matth:1.23.	A Virgin Shall be with Child etc.

Luke 2.34.35.   I know not a man——The Holy Ghost
                 Shall come upon Thee etc.
                 So, a wonderfull person
Isa: 9.6.   A Child born, Son Given etc. Mighty
                 God.
                 His Death
Danel. 9.26.   Messiah Shall be Cut off, not for Him-
                 self.
                 Such Things were Spoken of Christ, all
                 fulfilled etc.

5. This wonderfull Person appeard in the World 1770 Years ago. A Virgin Conceivd and bore a Son etc. As We have heard.

6. He Livd a most pure and holy Life—kept the Law of God perfectly—Did no Sin—Went About doing good. Preachd As never Man Spoke—Wrought Miracles—Heald Sick—raisd Dead—etc.

7. Was persecuted and put to Death, Crucified. Died in Our Stead—for our Sins. *Gave himself for Us—An Offering and Sac: For the Lord laid on him* [?Iniquity] *of us all.*

8. He was buried—laid in a Sepulchre, or Grave.

9. He rose from the Dead the Third day.

10. Went bodily up into Heaven, in presence of his Disciples. There he ever lives to make Intercession. Upon his Ascending He gave Gifts to his Church—Apostles—*Doctors* and Teachers—etc. *Lo I am With you* etc.

And now, As one of those Doctors I come, this day, to preach Christ—The Gospel of Christ unto You.

This Easter Sermon outline was included with the diaries in the Manuscript Collections of the Connecticut Historical Society.

Seventh Book 1770
Account of Indian Affairs at Narraganset

....

SEPTR. 24 [1770] . . . Preached at Mr. Deakes, (the School house,) to *Seven* Indians, from Isa: 55.6. *Seek ye the Lord* etc. Had Some degree of Freedom, and Some of the hearers expressd Satisfaction Afterwards. But there Seems, on the Whole, but Very little Encouragement to preach to these Indians. They Are generally So prejudicd, Jealous of Some ill design upon them, Careless, Slothfull etc. that there is no engaging of them to be Steady in attending on the means of Grace.[1]

Discoursd with *James Daniel* about gathering up his Brethren and Forming themselves into *Church-State*.[2] Told him the Form of our Covenant etc. He Seemd to like it Well, but Said his Brethren were Scattered and gone the most of them, And there Seemd but little *Likelihood* etc. . . .

[1] In a sense, of course, the Indians were realistic in perceiving "Some ill design upon them" for their resources were being whittled away rapidly and forever as a consequence of the assembly's decision to sell reservation property to repay Ninigret's debts (Bartlett 1861, VI: 564-65, 574-75, 589, 598-600). After Ninigret's death on November 12, 1769, Niles and several others petitioned the assembly to empower an Indian Council of nine men (mainly from Niles's faction) to transact tribal business and to protest the "Coronation of any King Queen or Prince of the said Tribe for the future" (Narragansett Indians No. 21, 1770; see also Wanton 1769). By September, 1770, however, a committeee appointed by the assembly brought the factions together to agree upon which particular lands to sell, and the tribe as a whole promised support for Esther, Thomas's sister, who reigned as Queen Sachem until her death in 1777 (Bartlett 1862, VII: 9-10, 15,

17-19; Campbell and LaFantasie 1978: 74; Chapin 1931: 102-3). The assembly denied an Indian request to appoint Narragansett justices of the peace but agreed that "no other of the Indian lands be thereafter sold on any pretence, whatever" (Bartlett 1862, VII: 18). The properties sold included Thomas's large house, an adjoining twenty-six acres, and the house of the late Sachem George Ninigret with about sixty acres (Ibid. 18). Finally, by August, 1773, the assembly sold enough land to discharge all Ninigret's debts and resolved "that all the lands now of right belonging to the said tribe, be secured to them; and that the same, or any part thereof, shall not, for the future, be liable to the payment of any debts" (Ibid. 215).

2 Since Daniel was associated with the Sachem's party, Fish here is inquiring into the possibility suggested in his December 4, 1769, note to Oliver, of extending his work among members of that faction.

OCTOBR. 15. 1770... Preachd at Mr. Deakes, Jno. 12.35. Middle Clause v. *Walk While ye have the Light lest Darkness come upon you.* But 4 Indians present. Yesterday the Indians had a meeting—Jno. Cooper from *Mohegan* preachd to about 200 Indians, as was judgd.[1] They Seem determind to discourage me from coming to preach to them, By Means of their party Spirit, prejudices, Jealousys, Groundless Objections from my Taking Money for preaching, Not Edifying of them, though I preach the Truth, they Say, and the like, Also their Ignorance and blindness as to the Advantages of the School and Gospel Ministry. I have but little hopes of Ever gaining their Attention. Visited *Ben Garret, Ammond,* and *Jno. Shattock* on Monday, and lodgd at Collo. *Chamlins. Tuesday* 16th Visited Queen *Esther.*[2] Talkd with them all upon their Neglect of Duty, and endeavourd to Stirr them up to it. Engagd the Queen to encourage her people to promote Learning and attend Lectures. Before Lecture [disco]ursd largely with *James Daniel* and [. . .] *Harry,* About gathering up their Scatterd Brethren and coming into Ch[urch]. Jno. *Shattock* renewd his desire or [ex]pressd his Freedom that I would have a Lecture at his house. Told him I was Willing to preach *there*, Next Lecture Save One. Proposd to *him* to Invite *Sam Niles* and his people to come to my Next Lecture, at *Deakes* And let Me Discourse with them: or if they did not Choose to come and hear Me, then that they would give me a Meeting after Lecture the Same Evening or day, Where they pleasd to Meet me, and let Me know why they forsook my Lecture. *Jno.* Engagd he would inform his Brethren.

....

1 John Cooper was a leading member of the nearby Mohegan of Connecticut (De Forest 1853: 461).

2 William Kenyon of Charlestown wrote a detailed account of Queen Esther's 1770 coronation ceremony (Boissevain 1975: 42-43; Chapin 1931: 102-3). Esther was succeeded in 1777 by her son George, who ruled briefly until he was killed in an accident. George was the last hereditary Narragansett Sachem. Thereafter the tribe was ruled by council, but the old factions remained.

Novr. 19. 1770 The School kept—but a few Schollars—a prospect of many this Winter. Preachd to 10 Indians, from Eph: 1.13. Had Some Freedom of Speech, but very little Sensibility—mournd My dry, dull Frame. Visited Young *Wm. Sachem*, Sick of a Consumption, After Lecture. Rode to Doctr. Babcocks (13 Miles,) after Sunset. Nothing Special appears, among the Indians, of their altering for the better. . . .

. . . Decr. 10. 1770 Preachd at Schoolhouse from Matth: 18.23-27. *He forgave him the Debt.* Had but 5 Indian Hearers and 3 English . . . besides Mr. Deakes Family. No Schollars to Day, and but few in a Steady Way. Indians in a Confusd, unsteady Situation. The Cellar, Under Great Room, all finishd, except Door. Tis 14 and 12 Feet dimensions. Has Cost, as Deake tells me, about 15 Dollars—Will cost Some more, perhaps 5 to finish. I Charged him to do it all as Cheap as possible. He said John Shattock refusd him the

Hinges (3 pair,) at his house. I told him I would look into the Affair and Clear the way. Went to Jno. Shattocks, to See his Son Jno., just gone with the Consumption. Discoursd him on Soul Affairs, endeavouring to Assist him, by referring to precious Scriptures. Took leave not expecting to See Any more, in this world.[1] Enquird of Jno. Shattock (The Father,) About the Hinges. Found 4 Setts, one large and 3 Smal. Mary Said, I had orderd the large Sett for entry door to the School Room, And the Other for Closet for Books. Jno. told me, the Indians were much out with Deake, faulting him for Cutting the School house to pieces, Meaning the making a Door out of his Dwelling room; to go abroad; for Making a Cellar; For not keeping School Steadily. Deake and I faulted for doing as We please about the House, Lands, Schoolmaster etc. etc. I told *John* to tell the Indians to meet me and Deake, next Lecture, and let us know their Grievances etc.

Went to Mr. *Parks* and lodgd there. Set out about Day, and desird Mr. Park to write Deake not to Use the Hinges at Johns, 'till I came down, that I might cut off Occasion of offence from the Indians.

At Mr. Eells' Met Letters from Esqr. Oliver and Doctor Eliot, giving Account of £17 Voted to Deake on Condition it would enable him to Clear his Debts. And 30 Blankets for Narraganset and Stonighton Indians.

---

[1] John Jr. died shortly afterwards on December 21, 1770, at the age of twenty-four. Fish wrote Wheelock in behalf of Shattock on January 30, 1771, to inform him of the death and to request him to inform the son's friends in Edinburgh and London (McCallum 1932: 214-18). Fish, who once employed John Jr. as master of the Stonington Pequot school, described him approvingly as "a very Serious, honest, faithfull man" but noted also that his religious sentiments "were Something of the *Separate* way" (Ibid. 215). John's last words to his father, who was a lay preacher among the Narragansett, were, "I have but a few minutes to Stay with you. Death has lost its Sting, and the Grave its

Victory—Father, hold out to the end—Be faithfull to Souls—be faithfull unto Death" (Ibid. 216). Wheelock considered Shattock to have been "a growing Saint" and noted sadly: "I esteem the loss to the tribe to be very great, and it seems to spread a melancholy gloom upon the general design that so many of the most likely and promising which I have educated are removed" (Ibid. 217).

JANY. 7. 1771 About 12 Schollars attend the School, and many more likely to come. Preachd, at the Schoolhouse, to about 60 Indians (Deake counted 57) on Isa: 8.20 *To the Law and to the Testimony* etc. Spoke with a measure of Freedom, And, (hope), of Sensibility. The Indians gave good Attention, And, by After Intelligence, have some reason to hope, were Edified.

After Lecture, desird that if any had ought to Say to me, (as I had heard of Some uneasiness,) they would take this Opportunity, and I would patiently hear and Mildly Answer.

John Shattock, (of *Sams* party,) Spake, and Said he approvd of my *Doctrine* or performances; but faulted "my Taking the *Government* out of the Indians hands", or Something like it. To which I replyd, There was no Foundation for the Charge—That it was wholly a Surmise—Tha[t] I was ready to Assist them in drawing up a Covenant, and Rules of Discipline or Government of their Church, According to their Own Sentiments or Notion, And to help them to the knowledge of what was Agreable to the holy Scriptures: but had no design, Desire or thought, of reducing them to Any *plan* of my own, nor to any other, without their Seeing and Consenting. Gave the Indians a Narrative of my Doings, in their Favour, from my First coming Among them; And that I meant nothing, but to do them All the good I could, by preaching the Truth, and Striving to reform their Evil Manners. On the Whole, Silenced John, And, believe, Satisfied the Indians present.

Endeavourd to heal an Unhappy difference between Mr. *Deake* and *John Daniel*, his Near Neighbour, who had Assaulted, Abusd and Threatend *Deake*: And hope Settled the Affair.

After Night, Visited poor *Margery*, Confind and unable to help her Self, for a Year or More, past.[1]

Took *Will Sachem*, one of the Indian Council, to pilote me through the woods. Understood by him, that I was much in favour with the Council. Proceeded from Margerys, through the woods, between 3 and 4 Miles, to Esqr. Yorks and lodgd there—late.[2] *Tuesday* 8. 9 o'Clock, Went to the Queen *Esthers* House, and met the Indian Council there, to take their Advice about Disposing of 20 Blankets, Granted by the Commissioners, to the most Needy Indians of the Narraganset Tribe, when they Should Arrive. They granted 30, for the Narraganset Indians and Stonington, to be dealt out at my Discretion. I ordered 10 to Stoningtn. and 20 to Narraganset.

The Council consisted of:

James Daniel	Willm. Sachem
Christr. Harry	David Philip and
Henry Harry	Thos. Sachem,
	the late Queens husband.[3]

List of the Names to whom Blankets were orderd, on the advice of the Council, and assistance of Mr. Deake, on whose Information I depended to form a Judgement of the most Needy and Suitable persons, Jany. 8. 1771.

....

[1] Probably Margery Aaron. See "List of Indians . . . Jany. 8. 1771."

[2] Probably Stanton York, a Freeman of Charlestown and an early communicant in Rev. Park's congregation (Bartlett 1861, VI: 142; Denison 1878: 69; Gilman 1869: 524-25; Parke 1872: 326-27).

[3] This council is a separate body from Niles's advisors who also considered themselves to be a council. Thomas Sachem was the *recent* queen's husband.

List of Indians to whom Blankets were orderd
per advice of Council ... Jany. 8. 1771,
At late Queen Esthers:

....

Men
Toby Coyass
Jo Coyass
Anthony Wilson
John Secutor
   Widows
Dorothy Dick
Mary Peter
Sarah Sampson
Margery Aaron
Abigail Hammer
Aunt Dorothy
Sarah Simons
Hannah Tias
Abigil. Boson
   no husband—
Hannah Cheets
   for her 2 Boys

The following Six Blankets were or-derd, to help Cloth the Children of Six Families, in order to fit them to Attend the School in Winter, their Parents being Spirited to Send them, but not able at present, to Cloth them. I say for the *Children*, and not for the *parents* Use viz: ˣ*Francis Hammer* a Fatherless Child, and weakly, living with her Grand-father James Danel., *Christopr. Harrys* Children, *Henry Harrys Children*, Danel. Harrys Ditto, Wm. Sachems, Ditto, David Philips Ditto.

I then Stirrd up the Council, as heads of the Tribe, to lay the Floors of the School room, above and be-low, and to put up the Partitions and Great Door. I also commended their Conduct, in joining Queen Esther, in Giving Deed of School house and Land, to Secure it for-ever to the Use of the School for Indians.

Next Lecture appointed at the Schoolhouse, 4 Weeks hence viz: 4 Feb : Mid day, and proposd to preach at Mar-gerys house immediatly after the public Lecture.

73

In Service and Journeying till *Tuesday* Night, About 9 o'Clock got home. *2 Days.*

FEB: 4. 1771. Found the School in a flourishing Condition—About 40 Schollars, writing Cyphering and reading, generally attend. Mr. Deake receivd, last Week, ½ Ream paper, ½ Doz. Spelling Books and 1 Bible, for the School, from Mr. *Pease* N. Port. He Sent but *One* Bible . . . .

....

Preachd to 40 or near 50 Indians, Some heads of Families, but chiefly young Indians, from Luke 16.31. *If thy hear not Moses and the prophets* etc. Had a good degree of Freedom—Dealt plainly with them and hope Some what faithfully.

Sunset went to Will *Sachems*, talkd to his Son Wm., near his End with a Consumption, but could get not a word from him—extremely Weak and I apprehend, no Sense of Death and Eternity. After prayer, turnd to a good number of Indians, chiefly Young, and Gave them A Serious Exhortation to improve their present day of Youth and Health, in Seeking God for his Grace to prepare them for Death.

After this, about day light in, Went to *Margerys*, about 3/4 Mile further East, Discoursd, prayd and preachd to the poor Afflicted and Confind old Woman, (in a very helpless Condition,) About 10 or 12 Indians being present, at her Wigwam.

Then rode about 7 Miles, to revd. Mr. Parks, in a pretty dark night and through Care of a kind watchfull providence, got there Well, (though Some what worried), before 9 o'Clock.

TUESDAY 5. FEB: a Very *cold, Windy* day, could not Set out early. However, Stemmd the Wind and Cold, and got home before Sunset, a good deal tird—a laborious Journey. The Lords name be praisd, got home, once more, and found my dear Family About house, as I left them.

....

FEB: 18. 1771. *Kit Harry* and one of the *Secutors*, At my house. *Secutor* told me that numbers of the Indian Children could read their Bibles Well, And that when they could get a *Bible* or Testament to read to their Parents at home, it enlightened and Convinced them greatly.[1] For When their Children read the Laws and Comands of Christ; that for Instance, *Owe no Man Any thing, but to love one Another*, The Children would Say to their Parents, "You dont do *So Father, Mother*", etc. And this Servd mightily to convince them of their *Sin* and their *Duty*. So that if the Children had Bibles to read at home, to their Parents, it would be a happy means of Spreading the Knowledge of the Gospel Among them.

N.B. Let the Commissioners know *This*, And ask them, if I may Order a *Bible* or *Testament* to be given to *Every Family*, where there is a Child who can read it distinctly to the parents?

[1] Mary Secutor attended Moor's Charity School in the late 1760s. Two letters from her to Wheelock, and two confessions regarding her conduct at school have been reprinted in McCallum (1932: 235-38).

MARCH 5. TUESDAY, . . . [1771]

Yesterday, being Monday the Day Appointed, bad Travelling by a deep Snow, did not Set out: but performd the Journey today.

Preachd to 12 Indians (only the Schollars, that day at School,) from 1 Jno. 3.24. *Hereby We know that he abideth in us, by the Spirit that he hath given us.* Had Freedom, but Wanted Solemnity and Sense of the Weighty Truths.

After Lecture, Attended closely to Mr. Deakes Affairs.
Enquird into the Ballance of Accounts with All his Creditors. He told Me he had lately Settled with a number of
them, and knew, to a peny, what he Owd them, which I
thought was Sufficient for me to know, As Agent for the
Commissioners, to See his Debts Dischargd. Wherefore I
told him, (to Save his Time in the School, now tis full,)
that he need only go and Settle with the rest of his Creditors
and take from Under their hands the Exact Ballance. Appointed Next Week, Wednesday, for him to bring the Account to my house. I told him, to Save his Time, I would
Settle for him, with Govr. *Ward*, which I did Next day.[1]

....

[1] Samuel Ward (1725-76), a Westerly resident, was chosen three
times as governor of Rhode Island colony (Biographical Cyclopedia
1881: 95; Goodwin 1907, II: 289-90n).

APRIL 1. MONDAY... [1771]
Preachd from Gal: 4.4.5. *When the Fullness of Time was
come* etc. To 8 Indians, but *one* Schollar at School today.

....

...MAY 6. 1771 Mr. Deake very dangerously Sick. No
School kept these few days past. Preached to 9 Indians and
About as many English, From Pm. 24.3.4. *Who Shall ascend
into the hill of the Lord* etc. Had a good measure of Freedom and, hope, Some Sensibility. Hearers gave Serious Attention. Perceivd afterwards, that the Discourse was to good
Acceptance, at least of White people. Blessed be the Lord.

....

Eighth Book 1771

Accounts—Indian Affairs Narraganset

....

MAY 27. 1771. Mr. Deake has kept no School for 3 Weeks, by reason of his Wifes Sickness. She is now better....

Preachd from Luke. 19.10. to Eleven (11) Indians. Nothing Special, at this Lecture and Journey, except that I engagd *Charles Daniel* to come up next Monday and Engage in keeping our School at Stonington, in Case I can provide him a house to keep at....[1]

[1] Charles, son of the Narragansett John Daniel, attended Moor's Charity School for at least two years (McCallum 1932: 231).

JUNE 17... No School, being no Schollars to day. But about 4 or 5 Schollars last Week. No Indians came to Lecture to day, Save Charles Danel. and he could not tarry; So had no Lecture. Determind not to loose my time, wholly, So went and visited Six Families, viz: *Jno. Daniels*, where I found 5 Indians; An Indian Woman Named *Mary* Jno., Sober—4 lay drunk, dead asleep. *Mary* told me they had a Drunken frolick last Night, and had no Sleep. I gave *Mary* a Solemn Exhortation, and bid her tell the poor Drunken Wretches, that I had been there and Seen them in that dolefull Condition, and would endeavour to See them again next Lecture, This day Four Weeks. James *Daniels*, Exhorted 5 Indians—Found *one*, a young Girl, almost gone with a Consumption, and Another Young Squaw, with a Bastard Child in her being. Exhorted them both, Suitably to their State.

Next, *James* Niles—only his Wife *Jerusha* at home. Had long discourse—Answerd her 2 grand Questions, viz: 1. Why I did not come to take Care of These Indians before, or till of Late Years. Answer I had no Call of Providence to preach to them and take Care of them, till about 6 years ago, and Shewd her particularly wherein. 2nd Question, Whether I had any Money for my Service Among them. Answer I have; And Justified it. The good people, over the Water, have Sent over Money to Commissioners *Boston*, on purpose for Ministers and Schoolmasters to the Indians: and Commissioners employd *me*; and so I had what providence had allotted for me, And twas the Will of God that I, and all ministers, that were devoted to the Ministry, Should be paid etc. etc.

Old Margery next—Near gone with Consumption. Exhorted, Instructed and encouragd her, to look to and hope in the Lord. 2 Indians here.

Jeremy Hazzard next—2 Young Indians here and 4 Children. Gave a Solemn Warning to these Two, a Man and Woman—The Man (*Jimmy Stanton* I Think his Name,) A light, Vain, Secure Fellow—Seemd to wax Sober at the Warning I gave him.

Jno. Shattocks next—His Wife and 2 Children, Son Jimmy and Daughter. Discoursd Suitably with Them—warned the Youths Against the Abominable Wickednesses of the Day and place. . . .

TUESDAY 18. A heavy Storm—had no Lecture here, as Appointd:

....

JULY 15. . . A rainy day—belated—hadnt time to visit the School, being above a Mile out of my Way: So cannot tell how it is with Mr. *Deake*. Only heard his Wife is Very Sick.

Preachd at John Shattocks to 16 Indians and Mustees; and about a Dozn. Whites; 6 of these English people live not far from the Ordinary place of my Lectures, Yet dont know that I ever Saw one of them before.

Had Considerable Freedom and was Somewhat engagd in establishing the holy Scriptures, as the only Rule of Faith and Manners—Containing all divine Truths, as in Jesus—Taught us by the True Spirit, the Spirit of God, And Shewd that the *True* Spirit refers us to What he has taught us *in his Word* for the trial of his own Influences, Operations and Teachings: And tis a grand Delusion for any to think that they are taught and guided by the Spirit of God *without* the Scriptures, or *So* as to render the holy Scriptures needless to them.

Hope that Some good was done. May God of his Mercy bless the word, and take the Glory.

....

AUGT. 12... Preachd at the School-House to about 9 or 10 Indians and negroes, from 1 Jno. 2.1. *My little Children these things write I unto you, that ye Sin not. And if any Man Sin We have An Advocate etc.* Revd. Mr. *Park*, Esqr. York and Wife and Daughter [?Gosset], also attended the Lecture, and Mrs. Deakes 2 Sisters, in the other room. I felt my Self in a very low Frame. Much discouragd about This Indian Mission, at Seeing the Indians So generally despise their privileges—Set no Store at All by the blessed Institution, of a preached Gospel. The Care that Christ takes of them, in Sending Messages of Grace to them, and ordering the holy Scriptures to be read, is Slighted by Almost All of them. They had rather follow That Ignorant, proud, conceited, Obstinate Teacher, poor *Sam Niles*, than Attend regular preaching of Sound Gospel Doctrine. Rather follow, Some of their work, others their pleasures, Idleness, Drunkenness, or any Way of Serving the Devil and their Lusts, than to Spend An hour or Two in hearing the precious Truths of the Gospel. I Saw Jno. *Danel.* and a *Squaw*, Mary John, I think her Name—(and they told me, Jno. Daniels Wife was there in like Condition,) At Wm. *Welch's*, half drunk. Askd them to Lecture, but they despisd it. However, was enabled to preach to the Edification and Counsel, I hope, of my Hearers. Mrs. *Deake* very Sick. School kept up. . . .

Septr. 2. . . Mrs. Deake is at the point of Death. No School been kept 3 Weeks back, on Account of her Sickness. Went from Mr. Deakes to Jno. Shattocks: there understood, that no Indians like to be at Lecture; by reason of a *Funeral* of a Child. Went back to the Meeting house 3 Miles, on the East Side of the great Pond—lost my road and went part of the way through the woods.[1] Indians not come. After ½ hour The Funeral came on. Corps carried into Meeting house. While Some dug the Grave, I enterd on a Free discourse, in the House, to about 20 Indians, opening Some points in principle and Practice, by Way of Conversation, to detect false Religion Among the Indians. Had Much *Freedom*, and hope did Some Service.

Then preachd to Above 30 Indians from Rom: 8.32. *He that Spared not his own Son, but Ditto him up for us all, how etc.*

Had Some degree of Freedom in preaching, and pressd Matters with Some Solemnity; but know not Whether Any Were Awakend to a Sense of their Sinfull practices, or disposd to return to my Ministry, in Attending Lectures.

....

1 Schoolhouse or Cocumpaug Pond.

Novr. 4. 1771... Preachd at Mr. Deakes to Elven Indians and a number of White people, chiefly Young people. Text—Mark 16.15.16 ves.—*Go ye into All the World and preach the Gospel* etc. Was favour'd with a good degree of Freedom and presence of Mind—with Some Sensibility and moving Address to the hearers, who Seem'd to a Very Serious Attention, and am not without hopes that Some good was done. Oh that these Indians might be Sensible of the Great Benefit of a preached Gospel—despise and neglect it no longer; but Attend to it, while they have Opportunity, lest the Things that concern their peace Should be hid from their Eyes.

The School Very thin—but 3 or 4 Indian Children now come. Their Parents Criminally Negligent—Will not get wood for the School, and their Naked or ragged Children cannot Sit in the Cold.

Appointed next Lecture at Jno. Shattocks, 4 Weeks hence. But James *Daniel* objected Against its being at *Shattocks*—Objected that Schoolhouse was in the Middle. So concluded to have it (after the next) at Deakes. But the next at Shattocks. ...

... Decr. 2. 1771 Preachd at *John Shattocks*, to about 20 Indians and Molattoes from Heb: 4.2. *For Unto us was the Gospel preached as Well as* etc. *Word preached did not profit* etc. Was favour'd with a measure of Freedom, and, I thought the *Word* made Some Impression on the Hearers. O that I could feel, in my Own Soul, more of the power and Efficacy of Divine Truth!

After Lecture, Inform'd the Indians that the Commissioners had Sent them a Number of Blankets, desiring they would inform me, by the Queens Council, concerning the most needy persons among them. Order'd, Said *Council*, allowing Some Heads, to Meet me, next Morning, 9 o'Clock, at Esqr. Yorks. Also, the Body of people being gone, (*James Daniel*, his Grandson *Charles Daniel*, And a few more Still there,) John *Shattock* informd me that the Indians were generally very Uneasy with Mr. Deake, and wanted to get rid of him. One Objection was, his taking English Schollars into School etc. Upon This I desird that the Whole Tribe would Attend the next Lecture, and let Me know What were the grounds of their uneasiness etc., in order to be removed. . . .

TUESDAY, DECR. 3. The *Queens Council* Came, and *Sam Niles, James Niles*, Jno. *Shattock* and Another Indian, to Afford Me Light about the most needy persons Among them, that the *Blankets* might be properly distributed.[1] They Behavd in a Very free and friendly manner, and Were united to [?a man], And Seemd Well Satisfyed in the following *distribution* of the Blankets, which, After I had particularly enquird into the Circumstances of Each person, was then made, viz; To

Toby Coyass	Abigil. Hammer
Jo Coyass	Aunt Dorothy
Anthony Wilson	Sarah Simons
John Secutor	Hannah Tias
Widows	*Abigail Boson*
Dorothy Dick	James Cuff
Mary Peter	Mercy James
Sarah Sampson	*Sarah Tom*

N.B. The Three last took the places of *Margery* Aaron, dead, *Francis Hammer*, dead, and *Hannah Cheats*, (whose children are put out,) to whom Blankets were Allowd, in our Settlement last Winter.

The following 5 Blankets were given to Cloth the Children of 5 Families, to fit them to come to the School, their Parents not being able, at present, to cloth them. viz:

Christophr. Harrys Children
Henry Harrys Ditto
Daniel Harrys Ditto
Wm. Sachems GrandChildren
David Philips Children

To All which, the Council and Heads, advisd and agreed, And I thought it fitting the Above Distribution Should be made.

Three Indians, viz: Kitr. Harry, Henry and (They engagd for their Brother,) Daniel Harry, offerd themselves to Fetch the Blankets, free of Charge, from *Stonignton* harbour. Accordingly I gave them An Order to Mr. Joseph Denison, Merchant, to deliver to them or Either of them *Twenty Blankets*, for the Use of *Narraganset* Indians, As Above Settled.[2] And Same day, drew order on Said Mr. Denison, to Send 2 Quire of good writing Paper to the Indian School at Narraganset, and Charge to my Account.

Past 2 o'Clock Set out for home in a bad Snow Storm. Stoppd at Mr. Parks—from there Sun about 3/4 hour high. Calld at Dr. Babks. and Mr. Eells's. Got Well home near nine o'Clock. Mercifully preservd from Falls and enabled to endure the Cold, and to go through the Fatigue of This Journey and Service, with life and Spirit—*Laus Deo*!

....

[1] Thus Fish consulted the leadership of the queen's and Niles's factions.

[2] Denison was a common family name in the Stonington and Westerly areas, and two Joseph Denisons (1707-95; 1735-85) lived in Stonington at this time (Wheeler 1900: 347, 350).

DECEMBR. 30. '71 Preachd at the School house to about 40 Indians from the 4th Chaptr. Nehemh: Spiritualizd Nehemiahs building the Walls of Jerusalem, And Shewd them how to build up the Church of God—how to oppose and withstand their Enemies, by the Armour mentiond. Eph:

6.11-18 which verses were paraphrasd and Improvd. Had usual Freedom and not altogether without Sensibility. But found great want of it, and of many other desirable Graces. Lord humble, quicken, Solemnize and Sanctifie thy poor Servant, I do beseech Thee!

After Lecture desird the Indians present to let me know the Grounds of their Uneasiness and Dislike, at their Schoolmaster, Mr. Deake, having before heard that they had found much Fault with him, and woud not Send their Children.

James Niles Objected 2 Things, viz: That he did not keep So many hours in a day, as he ought: And that he lost much of his Time. As to the First Objection or Complaint, I askd *James*, if he know how Many hours a Master ought, or was requird to keep in a Day? He told me he could not tell. I told him he ought to have known *that*, before he Objected. Then I told him, that 3 hours in a Forenoon and 3 in Afternoon, was ordinarily as long as needfull or required. And As to The *Second*, Mr. Deake told him, twas true, he had lost much of his Time through long and heavy Sickness in his Family; but that it was his own Loss, for he made it all up again.

Christophr. Harry, (not for himself, but in Behalf of Others,) Mentiond Mr. Deakes taking English Schollars, as a Fault complaind of: Which Sam Niles took up and Improvd to Mr. Deakes disadvantage, and also complaind of him for promoting his own Party and making a Division Among the Indians, much to their Damage.

To the *First*, (Taking English Children) Mr. Deake assurd them that he did not desire to take any at all; and that when he did, it was with a view and Design to Stirr up the Indians to Send their own Children: which had Sometimes been Attended with that effect. And that as soon as the Indians Sent their Children, in Such Numbers as to afford him Suitable employ, he dismissd all the English; And

Should not, along time, take any English Children into the School, among the Indians, to the prejudice of *their* Children, which I told them I Should dislike as much as they. And as to the *Second* Objection—promoting *Parties* etc., Mr. Deake told the Indians He knew not of his doing any thing to occasion Such a Complaint, unless it was, that when *Any* Party Among them desird him to *write* or do Any Business for them, he was always ready to Assist them, and when he had done, he Had nothing for his pains.

These were all the Objections that were made; And the Answers Above, Silencd them all; but whether they were any thing better Satisfyd, I cannot yet Say.

Left Mr. Deakes About Sunset, in design to go to Mr. Parks. A Small Snow This Afternoon, had hid the *Ice* (of which there is much, in the paths,) and made it Very Slippery. When I had travelld About 2½ Miles, being now dark, my Beast Slippd on a patch of Ice—Fell upon my leg and Thigh, and Shockd my Neck and Shoulders a little; but found, on rising, that no Bones were broke, neither my *Self* nor *Beast* any thing hurt. O what a Deliverance is this! What a great Mercy have I experiencd, as I was alone, in the Night and about 3/4 Miles from Esqr. Yorks, the nearest house. There I walkd on Foot. Lodgd there, and home next day by Collo. Pendletons, about 7 o'Clock night....[1]

[1] Colonel William Pendleton of Stonington (Wheeler 1900: 532).

... JANY. 27. 1772 Preachd, at the Schoolhouse, from Eph: 3.8. *Preach, among the Gentiles, the unsearchable riches of Christ.* Had a measure of Freedom, but, alas! Wanted Spirituality and a Sense of divine Truth—Don't know that the Word of God made any Impression on the hearts of Hearers—Have reason mourn my unsuccessfullness. However, as I endeavour to be faithfull in promoting the Redeemers Intrest, I will hope that Some Good is done, in Some respects or other.

The School is kept—about 20 Indian Schollars, in the Indians room, And Mrs. Deake Tends a number of English Children in her room.

After Lecture I exhorted the Indians (a number of old Indian Men being at Lecture,) to mend the Windows, as many Quarries were broke out, and the room Very Cold. Mr. Deake has not put forward the Petition and Door etc., As the Season is very Severe and the Days Short—waits for longer days.

No Talk, as I could learn, Among the Indians, respecting Any uneasiness, Since my last Journey. The Schollars want Bibles and Paper. One Indian (young Niles,) Askd for a Bible to be kept in his house. I intend to Ask direction of the Commissioners respecting Such a distribution of Bibles.

Set off About Sunset, for Mr. Parks, in Company with Mr. Jno. Park. Reachd there Safely Some time After day light in—kindly receivd, Entertaind and lodgd there.[1]

1 John Park (1742-1812) was the sixth of nine children born to Abigail and Joseph Park (Anonymous 1917: 16).

TUESDAY JAN: 28. At Mr. Parks Spent most of the Forenoon in writing Letters. Wrote to Mr. Peter Bourse N. *Port* for 12 Bibles and 4 Quires Paper for the Indian School here and promisd him An Order on Govr. Oliver for the pay on receiving his Account. Wrote another Letter to Doctor Wheelock respecting his Taking one of Mr. Deakes Sons in his School. Set out for home, reachd it Safely After Sunset. Severely Cold, and very Slippery, hard riding—Ground Chiefly bare, and hard as a Rock. Don't know that ever performd Journey to those Indians, in a more difficult Season. But was mercifully preservd and once more returnd home, in Safety and Found my Family Well and Tabernacle in peace. Blessed be God.

This Journey took me 2 Days.

... FEBY. 24. 1772 Reachd Mr. Deakes about 2 o'Clock. But 3 Indian Schollars to day at School—had about half a Score last Week and back. No Paper and in want of Bibles. ...

Preachd from Matth: 11.12. *The kingdom of heaven Suffers Violence and the Violent* etc. To 7 Indians and Some English Schollars—one reason why so few, Supposed to be the many Meetings they had last Week. From Wednesday to Fryday Met Among themselves: and From *Fryday* to *Monday* Mr. *Sampson Occum* was preaching and labouring with them, (Tis Said, very plainly and Faithfully,) So that they have had a Fullness.[1] And Also they had a *Funeral* to Attend today, which took off Some of my usual Hearers.

I found my Self a poor, barren, empty Creature, fitter to retire into Obscurity, And Spend the rest of my days in Silence, than Attempt to Speak publicly in the name of the Lord. Though was enabled, I trust, to deliver the Counsel of God, in a measure of Clearness and Seriousness. Lord Bless Thy Truths to *my own Soul*. Let *me* feel the Weight and Importance of Divine Truth and let not my few poor *hearers* Starve under my Ministry! I am much discouraged. God Seems not to own and bless my Labours. Oh that God woud take away all my Idols, and draw my heart After him; that I may come near to the Throne of Grace, and *pray* and *preach* with Life, Zeal, Power, and to the Edification of precious Souls. Oh that God would make me *Spiritual* in *State*, Frame and *Conversation*. Lord grant it, for Thy Mercys Sake Amen.

A Snow Storm and exceding bad travelling. Went to Mr. *Parks* and lodgd there.

1 Samson Occom (1723-92), a Connecticut Mohegan who converted in the Great Awakening, was a well-known preacher and schoolteacher among the Indians and English of his day (Blodgett 1935; Love 1899; Richardson 1933; Sprague 1858, III: 192-95).

TUESDAY, FEB: 25. A Most Violent Storm of Wind and Rain. Tarryd till About 3 o'Clock. Set out for home. Bought 3 Bibles of Doctr. Babcock for the Indians Narraganset which Were Chargd to me, I paying this Spring....

Lodgd at Mr. Eells's Tuesday night.

Wednesday bought 2 Qur. Paper of Cpt. Rhodes, and paid him Sh. 2/.

Reachd home to breakfast.

This Journey, for Rain, Wind and bad Travelling, exceded almost All that ever I had undertaken. But blessed be God, I got home perfectly Well.

The next Lecture at Narraganset, is to be Three Weeks hence, from last Monday....

...APR. 13. 1772 Mr. Deake not Well, days past and but An Uncertain School for Some Weeks. Settled Affairs with Mr. Deake respecting Cellar etc. to lay before Commissioners. Deliverd him 3 Bibles and 2 qr. paper, for the School, which I bought on my own credit. No Lecture this Time, as the Indians knew not of my Coming. Was hindred all last month, by bad Weather. Spent the Time in Visiting the Indians, at their Houses, from Jno. Secutors to Jno. Shattocks. Met with And Exhorted 30 Indians old and young. Was helped to Freedom and Some degree of Solemnity and Affection. Indians All Seemd thankfull and Some of them Affected with my Discourse.

MAY 11. 1772 No School kept last Week, nor now, for want of Schollars—not one Child Sent. Poverty, or Carelessness, or Some other Sad defect prevails Among Indians.

Mr. Deake has Receivd the ½ Thousd. Shingle Nails, which I bought and Sent him, but nothing done to Stop Leaks in the house, for want of Boards and Shingles, through hurry of Planting and oxen Weak.

Tis Supposd that many of the Indians would be glad the School was at an End.

Preachd to 13 Indians and a number of White people, from Jno. 14.6. I am the Way the Truth and the Life. *I am The Life*. Had a measure of Freedom, and was enabled to Open the Subject with Some Clearness; and would hope the poor Indians learnd Something. But alas! I know not What method to take, nor Argument or Motive to Use, to engage them to Attend the Lecture or regard the School. It Seems as if the Devil holds them fast in Chains.

Went to Jno. Shattocks—Busy at planting, but had no Thought of the Lecture. Pretended he had forgot all about it.

Visited Jemima York.[1] She Seems Almost gone with Consumption.

Lodgd at Revd. Mr. Parks. Engagd him to preach for me . . . when I expect D.V. to be at Boston.

Appointed the Next Lecture 4 Weeks hence, viz: Monday June 8th. Got home Tuesday Noon. In Service 1½ Day.

1 Perhaps a daughter of Anna and Stanton York, communicants in Park's church (Gilman 1869: 525; Parke 1872: 326).

To Revd. Mr. Fish

Charlestown the 13 of Jany. AD. 1773.
REVD. DEAR SIR.

Inasmuch as the Honourable Commissioners have appointed you their Agent, and Missionary to the Indians, whose care the School is more immediately under, that in regard to the poor Indians I find myself under obligations to acquaint you, Sir, with the present State of the School, together with some remarkable conduct of some of our Zealous separate brethren.

The sickness that has been of long continuance among the Indians has some what abated, that the vacancy closed the next day after your last Lector among them, and had ever since a pretty School. Some of the Indians are more Zealous to send their Children to School than what they have been for several years past. A testimony of this is, the Harry's (them noble Indians) have raised hands and cut and carted wood for the School, which is more than ever was done before by any of the Indians since the School House was built, though myself and their poor Children has greatly suffered for want of it. The Sachems party (as its called) and some of the principle Indians on the other side, are well satisfied with you, and myself. But some of our Zealous brethren since the School appears to be under more promising circumstances than what it has for a long time back, are like the troubled Seas when they cannot rest, whose waters cast up mire and dirt. They have used their Influence with the Indians to prevent their sending their Children to School; but finding this Impracticable, (as I am informed this evening) Minister Niles, John Shattock, with sundry others have become very Zealous in Favour of the School, and have got a letter wrote by some accurate penman filled with Charges against me, to have me removed from the School, and get another Master that will promote their religion. The Charges against are as followeth (Viz): Taking English Children to School, turning away the Indians Children from the School, don't keep my appointed Hours, write for the Sachem, with sundry other things which I can't enumerate at this time, (all which you will find to be false). Christopher Harry says that the parson Graves at New London is at the Bottom of it all, but how that is I can't say. Saml. Niles is a going to the Commissioners with the letter himself, and what the consequence will be I know not. I esteem it an honour to be Imployed by such good and honourable men as the Commissioners are, but this I know, that before I'll promote heresy and Enthusiasm in stead of Bible religion I will beg my Bread.

At the Indians meeting this day it was talked by Samel. Niles that, he didnot want any thing to do with you for you did not preach to the Indians when you came. You only said, the Prophets said So, and Paul said So, and Peter said so; you didnot Preach in the power of the holy Ghost, and say thus saith the Lord of hosts. However, I believe Saml. had more wit than let that be put in his letter.

It being late in the night I shall add no more then Just mention to you that my Wife was put to Bed about ten days ago, and is now in a very poor state of helth, not likely to recover soon.

In grateful rembrance of Friendship and Civilities, with kindest salutations to Mrs. Fish, I am sir, your most Humble Sert.

EDWARD DEAKE

Fish papers in the Manuscript Collections of the Connecticut Historical Society.

Tenth Book

Accounts of Indian Affairs 1773, '74. '75

....

MAY 10 [1773] .... Preachd at Deakes to his Family, Esqr. York and Wife, and to Three Indian Women.

Was Insensibly too long, in Sermon, upon Rom: 10.10. *With the heart man Believth unto Righteousness.* Though the Truths deliverd, I am perswaded, were Clear, great and Important, Yet was much mortified, through want of Brevity, Sense of Divine things, the Worth of Souls and tenderness of Affection.

Find, more evidently than ever, that the Indians, through an Implacable Temper, Inveterate and Growing prejudice, Are determined to break up both School and Lecture, by their non Attendance on Both, especially The *Lecture.*

David *Secutor* and his Wife came to Mr. Deakes on an Errand while I was there before Lecture, And, as if They came on purpose to Tantalize, Insult and Despise me, went off again Very Soon.

I came away more Discouragd than ever before—Thinking it more manifest than ever, that the Lord dos not Own Me, in this mission, and that he Will not bless my Ministry Among these Indians.

However, lest I be too unbelieving and too Sudden in my Conclusion, I think to try a little Longer. . . .

JUNE 7. 1773 Preachd at Mr. Deakes from Luke IId. 1-20. Expounded, but Insisted Chiefly on The Angels bringing *good Tidings of Great Joy.* Had a Measure of Freedom and Some Sense of divine things—hopd that God was graciously present With us. But 3 Indians, Women, to hear me. They Seemd to be well Satisfied. Was Sensibly Grievd that the Indians despise Their privileges, Set no Store by, nor make Any Account of the Ministry of the Word. Am concernd About my taking the public Money, and do So little Service. Advisd Deake to find out the true Cause of the Indians prejudices against Lecture and School, and write them down, by little and little, that I May See them. No Scollars nor School Since I was there last. . . .

. . . JULY 5. 1773 No Indians, at usual Time of their Coming, So I visited Sam Niles, James Niles and John Daniel. Sam not at home. Talkd with old Tobe Cowyass and Two Squaws there.[1] Tobe Said he had, Sometime ago, been home, (meaning, to Heaven). Had Seen the *Great God,* and that he was a Great Gentleman. Had Seen Jesus Christ, A handsome Man. Seen also a Multitude of Folks in Heaven, Resembling Butterflies of Many Colours, etc. Strange, Gross, Horrible Ideas and notions of the heavenly World! I corrected them as far As I then Could, and left them. Calld at James Niles's—had large talk with him. He Said Deake was not Faithfull and that I supported or Upheld him, therefore Indians would not hear Me, nor Send their Children to Deake etc., Which I endeavourd to Confute, denied the Charge and calld on him to prove it. I desird James to Attend Next Lecture and left word for Sam Niles to Come too, for I had Something Special to Say to him. Left Word at Sams House. Calld to See Jno. Daniel. His Wife deep in Liquor—Told me I might go off as Soon as I pleasd. Went forward and preachd at Deakes To 7 Indian Hearers. . . . Had Considerable Freedom and Some degree of Sensibility. Had Indian Man and his Wife Who never heard me before. . . .

---

¹ Cowyass was a variant spelling of Coheys.

. . . JULY 26. 1773 Preachd at Deakes from Pm. 63.1. *My Soul Thirsteth for Thee* etc. To 9 Indians, 5 of them Deakes Schollars and 4 Indian Women. One of the Squaws Showd uneasiness—Went out of Meeting. Told Deakes' Daughter (who went out After her) She had heard enough, She didnt want to hear Any more. What, Says She, "Cant that old Creature preach no better"? etc. As the most of my Indian Hearers, and Some English Schollars, were Children, and the Squaws (most of them) as Ignorant as the Children, I therefore endeavourd to feed them with Milk. Talkd in the most plain, easy and Familiar Manner in Shewing of them what this *Thirst* of Soul after consists in, or what is to be Understood by it; And have reason to think I gave a Scripture Account of the Doctrine.

But these poor Indians, not knowing the Bible, nor indeed paying any Regard to it—being Used to Noisy, Empty Exhortations, Visionary Imaginations, Sights of Christ *without* them, Impressions, outcrys etc. etc. have no knowledge of nor Relish for the plain Solid Truths of the Gospel.

There was not One Indian (besides Schollars) came, till after Meeting begun: Which Inclind Me to think of coming no more to preach to them for the present. But afterwards concluded to try once more . . . .

. . . AUGT. 23. 1773 Preachd at Mr. Deakes from 2 Cor: 3.5th to 8 Indians, and About 18 or 20 English, not That we are Sufficient of our selves etc. but our Sufficiency is of God.

Had Some Freedom in Thought and Expression, but alas! For my want of Spirituality. Oh that God would Clear my Duty, with respect to these Lectures!

But 3 Indian Schollars today, and not above 5 at Any Time of late. Calld at Ben Garrets and put him in Mind of his promise to Attend my Lecture. He came. Numbers of English gave out that they intended to come to this Lecture: but, Supposd, the Rain prevented them. I Stood too long in Sermon (a great Common Fault—O that I may Correct it for future) And hurt my Self....

... Octr. 4. 1773. Mr. Park preachd my Sixth Lecture in Course... I gone to N. Havn., And I preachd this day to 4 Indians (Mr. Park had 11.) from Rom: 5.12. *By one Man Sin Entred* etc. Had Usual Freedom of Speech, but little reallizing Sense of Divine Truths, and, fear, little Impression was made. Lord humble me for my barrenness and unsuccessfullness—Shew me what I shall do, and help Me.

Deake has but Very few Indian Schollars. Discoursd him on Many Things, particularly on his Improvising on Lords days, Sometimes, to a few Indians, Who desire it, With Consent and advice of Mr. Parks Church, Which I consented to, provided he gos no further than a private Brother may do.

Left, in writing, My proposal and Desire, that Sam Niles, Michal Tobe, Henry Harry and Chtr. Harry, Meet Me at Deakes Next Lecture and Consult about proper Indians to Receive Blankets this Fall....

... Octr. 15. 1773 Preachd from Rom: 5.12. The Improvement of Last Lecture here. Had Some New Hearers, at least not Usually here, Ten in all. Mr. Park attended the Lecture, and talkd Very Seriously and Faithfully to the Indians, After Lecture, on their Neglecting and Despising the Means of Grace, According to Gospel Appointment. Told them that the Teachings and Means which they had, were not of God—Came not from heaven, and would never lead them there. Consulted those Indians, that were present, about Suitable Objects to receive the Blankets: And Concluded on 17. One has had a Blanket, and 2 blankets more not yet disposd of. Left in Writing my request and order, that the Indians mentiond, Should meet me at the School-house, This day 3 Weeks, viz: 8th Novr. to Receive their Blankets, which the Indians are to Send for to my house, before Said day. . . .

. . . Novr. 8. 1773 . . . Went down and preachd to a large Number of Indians, I judgd, between 40. and 50, but forgot to Count them. Text Luke 14.21.'2.'3 *Then the Master of the house being Angry, Said to his Servant, go out quickly into the Streets and Lanes of the City, and bring hither the poor, and the Maimed, halt and blind* etc. Had much Freedom and Some Sense of the Truths. Indians gave Decent Attention. Who knows but they may be Inducd to come *to hear the Word, next* Lecture, as they doubtless came to *This*, that they might *Receive Blankets.* Having before informd my Self of the most needy and proper Objects to bestow the Blankets upon, I calld them all over after Lecture, This Time, And Observd to the Indians the particular State of Each Indian, to Whom I gave the Blankets, that *they* might See the ground of my Conduct, in the Distribution, to Cut off All Occasion of offence. The Most of the Indians were there, in person, to receive their Blankets, or Sent; and So all, but two, had them this day.

Distrubtion of Blankets Sent by the Commissioners from Boston to the Indians at Narraganset. . .

June 4. 1773. Receivd from Governr. Oliver of Boston, Two Packs of Blankets, Which, as he writes me, are Supposd to contain 15 Blankets in a Pack. . . .

JUNE 14. Sent by Benja. Garret, to Care of Edwd. Deake one Blanket to Abiga. Hammer, who lost all She had, by Fire.

	Blankets
To Abigail Hammer	1

SEPR. 7.

To Sarah Dick Stonington Indian for Charles Danel. Master, for Covering— Lent for present	1

NOVR. 8. 1773. Distributed 19 Blankets to the Indians at Narragansett, (one being given before to Abigail Hammer Above) In the following manner, viz:

To

Betty Queen, Widow, poor	1
Sarah Tom, Widow Lame	1
Jo Coyhaz—Lame, a Cripple	1
Dorothy Weesicump, old and blind	1
Widw. Ammons Children	1
Patience Anthony, blind	1
Aunt Dorothy—Blind	1
Abigail Boson—Blind, almost	1
Sarah Michal, old and Lame	1
Sarah Rogers, old and poor	1
Sarah Potheag,—Lame	1
Deborah Skeesucks, Blind	1
Hannah Lewis—Lame	1
Jenne Secutter—Widow, Poor	1
Dinah Mortar, old, poor	1
Sarah Simon, Widow, poor	1
Hannah Tyn[?es], Lame, poor	1
Kit Harrys Children, to Cloth them, that they might come to School	1

Doctor Harry, For fetching the Blankets from
my house   1
All which, with the one on the other Side given
to Abigil. Hammer, amount to   20

And having Distributed all the Blankets as Above, I re-
minded the Indians of their Duty, to render Thanks first
to God, the Great Giver of all good things, And then to
their pious Friends, beyound the Seas, Whose hearts and
hands the Lord had opend, to bestow So Much of their
Substance to Charitable Uses, By Which Means These Indians had Schools to Instruct their Children, A Preached
Gospel to feed their Souls with knowledge and Understanding, and Clothing to cover and Warm their Bodys. And if
they neglected and Abused Any of these great Favours and
kindnesses, God would be Angry with them and punish
them for their Abuse.

Hereupon, (Among many other things) I invited them
to Come to my Next Lecture, (appointed 5 Weeks hence:)
but if they *would* not or *could* not attend it, I desird that
they Who feard God and regarded Religion, woud pray for
me, that God would be with me and Enable me to do his
Service faithfully.

Deake has few or no Indian Schollars, and things look
dark upon the School. *Deake* also told me, that *Sam Niles*
and his party had a Meeting, to petition the Assembly of
Rhode Island, to put *him* and *me* down, because We had
taken the School from the Indians, and given it to the
English Children. An Absolute Falshood.

But the Harrys opposd the motion, and put them by
from their purpose. *Kit Harry* told me, That the reason of
Sam Niles and his party Leaving My Lecture, was, Because
I Said, "That if they did not know, or could not read, the
Bible, They could not be converted," (or to that effect,)

And thence they concluded, that, in my Opinion, They Were All going to hell. I told him, it was not So; but my Opinion was, And, doubtless, I had Spoke to this Effect, that the Spirit of God converts Sinners by his *Word* of *Truth*—The *Truth* that is in the *Bible*. And if they *cant read* the *Bible*, yet if they are converted, tis done by *Bible Truth*. So that the Spirit of God dos teach them *Bible Truths*, though they cannot read, and So, may not know that they are in the Bible. Of his own Will begat he us *With the Word of Truth.*

If these poor people were led and guided by the Spirit of God, the Spirit of Truth, would they Separate from me for Such a Saying? And never tell me of it neither? Never talk with me about Such a great point, to get light upon the Subject, fearing lest they Should be deceivd and perish! Surely Tis not the Spirit of Christ, but of Antichrist that influences them thus to Conduct. . . .

To The Honorable Andrew Oliver Esquire
/ Lieutenant Governor / Boston

Stonington 10th Novr. 1773

HONOURED SIR,

The special Occasion of my writing so soon, after a large Letter, by Mr. Babcock, is an unhappy Event, which has, Since that, taken place, at our Indian School, in Stonington.

Charles Daniel, of the Narraganset Tribe, who has for Some time past, kept the School here, to good Acceptance, has lately took to hard drinking, frolicking and loosing his time; at least it has but lately come to my knowledge. Upon enquiry, I found the report true; and indeed he himself ingenuously ownd it: but gave me no grounds to expect a thorough Reformation. So I thought it duty to dismiss him from our Service. I am Sorry for the Occasion, as he is a very likely, well accomplishd Young Indian. However, he had made out Two Months[x] in the School, (Since the end of the last Quarter, which I have drawn for, and has been paid,) before I dismissd him; which, being his due, I have drawn thus early, as per order accompanying. I think to wait till our New School house here is finishd, before I look out for another Master.

I take this Opportunity to inform Your *Honor*, that I have, this Week, distributed 20 Blankets, among the most Indigent of the Charlestown Indians, (the Other Ten for Stonington,) —had near about 40 Indians at Lecture, who appeard to be well pleasd; but whether with the *Truths* that they heard, or the *Blankets* they Receivd, their future Conduct, perhaps, may discover.

I think 'twas your *Honors* Order, in a former Letter, that I should transmit the Names of the Indians, to whom I gave the Blankets, for the use of the Honorable Commissioners. I have entred a List of the Receivers, on the other Side, with a Touch of their Special Situation, as the Ground of my Conduct.

I am much concernd about the Subject and Issue of my Last Letter, respecting Mr. *Deakes* School. I shall thankfully receive any Correction that the Honorable Board shall See cause to make. Or if what I offerd, on the difficult Subject, be Acceptable, their Approbation would relieve me of a pressure, which the Simplicity of my doings could not wholly prevent.

Most humble and Dutifull Regards to the Honorable Commissioners, and allow me to Subscribe, with great re-

[x]wanting ½ Day

spect, Your Honors most Obedient, and most humble Servant

JOSEPH FISH

List of the Indians who receivd Blankets,
in the Last Distribution, at Charlestown Novr. 8. 1773—

Abigail Hammer,	1	Lost her Wigwam and all She had, by Fire.
Betty Queen,	1	A Widow and poor.
Sarah Tom,	1	Widow and Lame.
Jo Coyhaz	1	Lame, a Cripple.
Dorothy Weesicumps.	1	Old and blind.
Widow Ammons Children	1	poor.
Patience Anthony,	1	Blind.
Aunt Dorothy,	1	Blind.
Abigail Boson	1	Almost blind.
Sarah Michal	1	Old and lame
Sarah Rogers	1	Old and poor
Sarah Potheag,	1	Lame
Deborah Skeesucks	1	Blind.
Hannah Lewis	1	Lame.
Jinny Secutor.	1	Widow, Poor
Dinah Mortar,	1	Old, and poor
Sarah Simon,	1	Widow, by Sickness; poor
Hannah Ty[?nes],	1	Lame and poor.
Kit Harry,	1	To cloth his naked Children, that they might come to School.
Doctor Harry,	1	Given him as a Recompence for fetching the Blankets 15 Miles.

By Your Honors most humble Servant

JOSEPH FISH

[*Inserted in left margin*:] Copy, not Verbatim, but for Substance the Same. Also, In the Letter Sent, I added Something about a Draft on Govr. Oliver. . . .

[*Inserted inverted in right corner of envelope*:] Copy, in part, my Letter to Govr. Oliver on Dismissing Charles Danil, and other Things. Novr. 30. 1773. Transcribd and Sent.

Fish papers in the Manuscript Collections of the Connecticut Historical Society.

. . . DECR. 13. 1773. . . Preachd at Mr. Deakes to 4 Indians and a few White people, Math: 6.21. *Where Your Treasure is, there will Your Heart be also.* A plain profitable discourse, but had little Sense of the Truths, or Spirituality of Frame. Oh that God would heal the Deadness of Soul I, too often, labour under. Deake has but one Indian Schollar as Yet—hopes for *More* When Winter Shuts in. Concluded to get (i.e. bespeak) Some Bibles, about 6, 8, or 10. About 1½ Doz. Spelling books, and ½ Doz. Primmers, and Some paper, which last I have. Told Deake that for the Future, Whatever Books I Sent or procurd for the School, must lie there for its Use, and by no means be carried out. And if Any Indians Wanted Books for their Familys Use, they must Apply to me, and I would help them to what is proper. . . .

. . . JANY. 10. 1774 Preachd at Mr. Deakes from Math: 20.6.7. *Why Stand ye here all the Day Idle etc.* to Eleven Indians, Women and Scollars. Had a Measure of Freedom and (I dare not Say but) Some Sensibility. Oh that God would be pleasd, of his great Mercy, to Send Me into his Vineyard and Employ all the Powers of my Whole Man, in Service, for the Salvation of Indians and all others, to whom he allows Me, At any time, to preach: And that, by his Grace,

I may be enabled So to keep my own Vineyard, that I may not be Cast away my Self! So help me, Lord Jesus, Amen!

Met with Nothing Special. Deake has 8 or 9 Indian Scholars. Carryd down, of my Own, 3 Quire Paper 3/. and also 2 Bibles. They want Books. I bought 1 Doz: Spelling Books and ½ Doz: Primmers for the Narraganset Indian School, and left them at Dr. Babcocks to be Sent to Revd. Mr. Park, and Desird the Doctr. to Send them 8 Bibles more, When he Should have them. . . .

. . . FEB: 7. 1774 Preachd at Mr. Deakes to 24 Indians of Which about ½ Doz. came on purpose to the Lecture, the Rest belongd to the School. Text 2 Cor: 8.9. *Ye know the Grace of our Lord J. Cht. Who though he was rich Yet for Your Sake he became poor, that Ye through his poverty Might be rich.* A Subject that I had only Thought up on the Evening before but had not writ Any Thing. Spoke with Some degree of Freedom, but a humbling Sense of Dryness and want of Affection and Solemnity. Oh that I could *Believe* and *Trust* more firmly, When I feel a want of Sense. Nothing Special, at This Lecture. Deake has an Agreable School—About 25 Indian Children and Youths, Male and Female, Which behave Orderly and learn Well. They Want Bibles, greatly. Enquird at Dr. Babcocks, but he has none. Appointed next Lecture 4 Weeks hence viz: 7 March. . . .

. . . MARCH 7. 1774 Preachd at Mr. Deakes to 8 Indians from Rom: 10.10 *With the heart man believeth unto Righteousness and with the Mouth Confession* etc. Glossd on preeceeding [?Canticle]: Shewing that J. Christ is nigh us—present in his Word, i.e. The Word of Faith or Gospel which his Ministers preach, therefore as near and ready at hand to

hear and help poor Sinners, As if on Earth. Had a Measure
of Freedom in Thought and Expression, but yet labourd
in utterance through a Cold etc. and was too long, to the
Injury of my Health and, I fear, to the Hearers, which
were 8 Indians. Had but little Sense or Affection, which
made my Labours harder Still, and I fear had no Success.
Dont know that Any Impression was made on Hearers, by
the great Truths that Were deliverd. Lord humble me,
Quicken, help, Teach me Duty respecting this Mission to
these Indians. Deake has now but a Smal School—Full
enough all Winter, but now they most all Dispersd....

APR. 4... Through Some Misinformation, I was not ex-
pected—Deake not at home, And but one Indian Girl there.
So I left, in writing, that D.V. I would be *there* This day 5
Weeks viz: 9 May—and give them a Lecture. Then Went a
Visiting among the Indians.

At George's, A Molatto that lives with late King *Toms*
ejected Squaw, I Met with 5 Indians:[1] one of them, *Betty*
Danel. Much in Drink, railing at Mr. *Deake* and *Me* and
Speaking illy of others. Another Squaw, Asleep on the Bed.
The Other Three Sober, to Appearance. I Seriously ex-
horted them all.

At Wm. Sachems, found 5 Indians, old and young, whom
I Exhorted and warned to Flee from wrath to Come.

At *Jo Cousins*, discoursd largely with him, on his Hope
of Eternal Life, on his Living So Contented, without the
Bible and Preached Gospel.

At John Shattucks, Met with 4 Indians, viz: Shattucks
Wife, Aunt Doroty, and Jno. Shattucks Son and Daughter.
Discoursed freely and particularly with them All, About
their Spiritual Affairs. In All I met with 16 Indians,
and, hope, was Somewhat Serviceable to them, in General.
Deake has but One Schollar that, of late, Steadily Attends

the School. I found Some of the Indians Sadly prejudiced Against Deake, And fear they Can never be reconcild to him.

[1] Mary Whitfield, alias Moll Drummer, married Ninigret in 1761, and they later divorced (Chapin 1931: 102).

... MAY 9. Preachd to 8 Indians, at Schoolhouse, from Heb: 12. 14. *Follow holiness, without which etc.* Had considerable Freedom, and, in a Measure, deliverd from that dryness and Insensibility which, too often, attends me. Blessed be God for the least help in my work, under So many Discouragements. Askd *Sarah,* an old Indian Woman, who commonly attends my Lecture, if She knew the Reason why the Indians Were So generally Set against coming to My Lecture? She told me, She Supposd they dare not come; for *Sam Niles* warnd and Solemnly Chargd them, not to hear Any of Our Ministers, that wore great White Wigs—that none were Devils, but the Angels etc.: the meaning of which I did not Understand.[1]

The few Indians present, Seemd to be Suited, and, I hope, profitted, by the Sermon. Deake has had no Schollars, Since Last Lecture. . . .

[1] According to one of Fish's North Stonington parishioners, "his well-adjusted wig gave the *crowning* beauty to his person" (Hubbell 1863: 10).

... MAY 30. 1774 Monday, Met with much Difficulty and Toil in getting there, by reason of Roads Turnd and Fencd up. Preachd at Deakes—had but 3 Indian Hearers, 1 old Woman and 2 Boys, Deakes Schollars. Text Jno. 3.19. *This is the Condemnation* etc. only the 4th and [. . .] Head— Solemn Truths, And not without Some Sensibility. Met with Ephm. *Coyass.* Enquird the Reason of his Not Attending Lecture? He told Me, The Indians were New Lights and

I Presbyterian, So did not Agree. Besides, I took Money, (he Said) for preaching: which he Thought was wrong *etc.* I endeavourd to Inform and Satisfie him. Told Me he Would come hear Me preach, the Next time: but I scarce believe him. Deake but 2 Schollars. Indians, Some of them, Affronted because I orderd the School Books to lie in the School for its use, and not carryd home to return no more, So get new Supplies every Year....

... JUNE 27. 1774 Being Somewhat Late, 2 Indian Hearers just gone away. Calld them back, with blowing the Shell. Being desird to Visit an Indian Woman, *Francis*, very low with Consumption, the Indians present Consenting, We Went 1½ Mile further, and held Lecture at the Sick Womans. Found her Very low, no Hopes of Recovery. Talk freely with her on the State of her Soul and Spiritual Affairs, which She Seemd Free to hear, and kindly receivd. Told Me She knew not that ever She had experiencd a Change of heart; but Seemd not much Awakend with a Sense of danger of perishing. Though Appeard Serious, and Thankfull for Instructions on Soul Affairs, and for the Sermon.

Preachd at her *Hut*, from 1 Pet: 2.7. To you *that believe he is precious.* 7 Hearers Indians. Appointd next Lecture at *Deakes* or Any private Indian House, if Desird, which Mr. Deake was to Acquaint himself and me with Next Lecture 4 Weeks hence, July 25. 4 or 5 Indian Schollars, commonly! Lodgd at Mr. Parks. Home Tuesday noon. In Service 1½ Day.

... JULY 25. 1774. Preachd at Francis's house from the 23d Numb: 10 v. *Let me Die the Death of the Righteous, and let my last End like his.* To 7 Indian Hearers. Had Some Degree of Freedom, but wanted Fervor and Solemnity. Was, rather Light, Dry and Empty as Chaff. O Lord humble me, and pray hasten to Quicken and excite in Zeal for thy great *name.*

Deakes School as thin as ever. His Difficulties very great and Discouraging. Being pressd for want of Two Dollars to pay his Rate, I lent him Two = 12/0—To be paid My next Journey. Am almost Discouraged. Fear I Shall never do them Any Good. . . .

. . . AUGT. 22. 1774 Preachd at Schoolhouse from 1 Pet: 1.5. *Who are kept by the Power of God etc.* To 5 Indian Hearers, Mr. Deakes Family and one Church. Believe the Indians in General Are determined not to hear Me Any More. Many of the Heads of the Tribe (and *Sam Niles* for one,) are gone off, with a view to Settle beyound Albany.[1]

The Lord orders all Events right, and if tis best and his Will, it looks as if it might be most for the Intrest of Religion here, if they return to Us no more. But Alas for the Indians! Where they Settle, if they Spread their False Religion. . . .

[1] In the early 1770s Samson Occom and his son-in-law Joseph Johnson began to plan an emigration of New England Indians to northern New York, where land was still abundant and where they could reestablish themselves apart from the demoralizing influences of the old frontier. After considerable discussion, in which the New England Indians described their powerlessness and poverty, the Sachems of the Oneida gave them a deed dated October 4, 1774, for a considerable tract of land where, the following spring, a small group of Mohegan, Narragansett, and Montauk began settlement of the Brothertown community (Blodgett 1935: 138-99; Hamilton and Corey 1962, XIII: 683-85; Love 1899: 207-30).

. . . MONDAY Sepr. 26. '74 Preachd at Mr. Deakes to only 2 Indians and Deakes Family, from Rom: 8.32d *He that Spared not his Own Son etc.* As my Coming at This Time was a little Uncertain, tis Supposd that a few of my usual

Hearers Were Absent on that Account. Mr. Deake Intends
to Phalmo. Cape Bay about 3 Weeks hence, and desires to
go in Character of a Preacher. On Which Account he Went
with me to Mr. Parks, Where Mr. Park and I Signd a Cer-
tificate of his regular Standing in the Church, Christian
Life and Conversation, Imploy in the Indian School, Oc-
casionally Instructing the Indians in the Christian Religion, Measure of Ministerial Gifts etc.: Which We Were of
opi[ni]on Recommended him to the Examination of the
Rhode Island Association of Ministers or any other etc. . . .

. . . Octobr. 24. Monday. . . Met Mr. Park at Mr. Deakes,
but no Indians, not one came. Mr. Deake Absent on long
Journey to Phalmouth, So no School. Mrs. Deake left
poorly, as to Provisions, and tenderly Affected; So I gave
her all the Money I had, about 16 Coppers.

Waited till Middle afternoon and no Indians Appearing,
concluded to Spend rest of the Day in Visiting the Indians.
Visited a little Indian Hut, near Grinnals; And Talkd with
and Exhorted 4 Children.

Visited David Secutor. Met with Flora, Hammonds
Widow—Discoursd Freely. Found her a Christian Woman,
but ownd and Lamented her Departure from God. Wept
Tenderly—Said She had not met with Any thing, a long
time, that took hold of her heart, like This Conversation.
Encouragd me She would attend next Lecture. Very Thankfull that I came in to See her. I then Talkd tenderly (as
with *Flora*,) to David Secutors Wife, abed with lying in.
The Talk Seemd to take hold of *her*. She Thankd me for
coming in to See her. Exhorted 4 Indians at This house.

Then Went to one Abrahams (I think his Name is) by
the High Way. Found their Daughter, Young James Daniels Wife. Discoursd with her About Affairs of her Soul and
religion. Found She Could read Very Well, upon Tryal—

but She had no Bible, Testament nor Psalter, nor Other Book. I told her I would give her a Bible, the Next Lecture, Which She Said She would Attend 4 Weeks hence. Then Visited *Doctor Harry*. Discoursd freely with him. Professd himself a Christian, but Could not read, but Said his Daughter Could. I told him he Should Call her to read the Word of God to the Family, every Night and Morning, when he performd Family Prayer. He told me that he Usd to pray with his Family, but had Neglected it of late. I admonishd and Excited him to his Duty. Turnd my Discourse to his Wife. She Said She could not tell What She Was— Sometimes Thought She was a Christian; but then Again doubted of it, her *Heart* was So Wicked. It was Such a *Plaguy Thing* (or to that effect) She knew not What to do with it, nor What to make of her Self. Discoursed here with 3 Indians. . . .

. . . Novr. 21. 1774 Calld at Ben Garrets, he absent—Exhorted his Wife and a Child. Went to the Schoolhouse. No Indians come to Lecture, nor any expected. Went to Visit at their houses. Calld to See *Jno. Daniel*; Exhorted him to his Duty—Expostulated with him about his Contempt of Christ, in refusing to hear his Gospel preachd, at the Next Door. Went to the Indian Meeting house, the Funeral of a Child being just over. Found 12 Indians at James Niles's, 3 of Whom went in there on My Invitation. I instructed them in Several points of Divinity, particularly About Satans Devices, and Transforming himself into An Angel of Light. Shewd them Where in Satan was now deceiving of them in the Form of a good Angel, by resting of them upon Inward Experiences; Revelations, Dreams, Impressions etc., Suggesting to them and perswading of them that they have their Religion directly from heaven; And So have a purer Religion than Standing Ministers Teach, (N.B. not *these words,* but purporting as Much). And upon it, they Neglect the *Bible,* in their houses and public Meetings; the Bible, by Which All of their Revelations and Christian Experiences are to be tryd, is Neglected and Despisd, which is one Evidence that Satan is deceving of them: for Christ Jesus resisted, Confuted and Confounded the Devil, only by Bible Truths. Therefore the Devil hates the Bible. Also, that Satan has a hand in Stirring Up *Sam Niles* their Teacher, to warn and Charge them not to hear Me preach, etc. etc. etc. *Doctor Harry,* present, told me, Afterwards, I Struck them in a Sore place—that they All Confessd, What I told them was True. Went to *Deakes* where I met with, and Exhorted 6 More Indians, from Our Saviours words, *Strive to Enter in at the Strait Gate.* In This Journey had Opportunity to Discourse to 22 Indians. . . .

. . . DECR. 19. 1774 Preachd at Mr. Deakes to 3 Indians, on 1 Peter 2.2. *As new Born Babes desire the Sincere Milk of the word that ye May grow thereby.* Discoursd with Some what of Freedom, and, hope, not entirely without Sensibility. But the Indians remain Indisposd to hear Me. A Publick Training, This day, at Mr. Champlins Tavern, Suppose, hindred Some few from attending Lecture. Mr. *Deake* has no Schollars as Yet: but Expects a Number, in a few days. With Some little prospect of his Schollars to be my Hearers, Appointed Next Lecture 4 Weeks hence, as Usual, viz: Jany. 16. 1775.

Wrote a Letter to *Sam Niles* to let him know I had frequently heard of his Charging the Indians not to come and hear Me preach: Which, if true, I had right to know what it was for, and twas his Duty as a Christian to come and Tell me. Put him in Mind of Christs Command, To go and tell a Brother his Fault, if he Trespassed Against him. Told him I was ready to Confess my Fault, if guilty of Any: but if not, 'twas Wicked in him to try to hinder the Indians from hearing the Gospel preached by Me. That I had been to his house to talk with him upon This affair, but he was not at home. Desird him to Meet Me at Deakes This day 4 Weeks, or at his Brother James Niles's, that We might come to a Christian Settlement of the Matter. But if he refusd to meet and talk with Me about it, he ought to Think how he Shoud answer it at the Bar of Jesus Christ, At the Last day, for endeavouring to hinder the Usefullness of one of his Ministers, by Speaking Against him behind his back. Signd, your Friend and Servt.—J Fish

N. B. The Letter was to the Above Import and in near the same words, as I remember.

....

JANY. 16. 1775. At The Schoolhouse Found a Full School—20 or 25 Indian Children and Youths, and 5 English. 20 Indian Schollars This day and 10 Indians more came to Lecture. Preachd to 30 Indians, from Matth: 11.17. *We have Piped Unto you and ye have not danced: we have mourned Unto You and ye have not Lamented.* Had (Through the Goodness of God,) a Measure of Freedom and Some Sense of divine Things. The Indians appeard to take Some Notice of what was Said to them. Hope I was enabled to be Somewhat *Faith*full, in Reproving them for their Contempt of the Gospel, and Reflections cast up on Christs Ministers, and refusing to hear them, as well as their Sensual Wicked way of Living. O that God would graciously please to work upon their Hearts, and bring them to Repentance. Who Can tell!

Heard That *Sam* Niles Receivd and heard my Letter read to him, And took no further Notice of it, than to Laugh at it.

....

FEBY. 13. 1775. Preachd at Mr. Deakes on Tit: 2.11-15 *For the Grace of God that bringeth Salvation* To 32 Indians— Paraphrasd on those words and made familiar Observations by Way of Application, as I went on. Previously meditated on the Words, but nothing writ. Had Considerable Freedom, and Enlargement, and Hope Some good was done.

Mr. Deake has a large School, of above 40 Indian Scholars, Who Seem Very industrious in trying to learn. They make good proficiency, (as Deake informs me) And will hopefully get much profit this Winter.

....

MARCH 13. 1775. The Indian Schollars begin to leave the School, the Weather being good for work. But about 10 or a Dozen.

Preachd at Mr. Deakes to Eleven Indians from Tit: 2.14. *Who gave him Self for, to redeem* us etc. Had a Measure of Freedom and Spake with plainness; but know not of any Impression on the hearts of *Hearers*; Among whom was James Niles Junr. Had much free talk with him after Lecture—found him a very Sensible Man and one of Sam Niles's Church, but Very far from being of *Sams* Spirit or way of Conduct. He faults them much on Many Accounts, especially for their Want of Discipline and *Rule* of Conduct, *which* indeed they have not: but behave after a Confused, Inconfident Manner.

They have Censurd him, but Are not Able to prove Any Fault, or Censurable Evil upon him. He is About leaving of them And going to the Indians at *Oneida.* . . .

. . . APR. 17. 1775. My Journey to N. Haven the 10th put off Lecture to this day. Preachd at Mr. Deakes, to 2 Indian

Women and 1 Indian Boy, all the Schollar that Deake has now. Text Math: 25.46. Handled the Canticle from v. 31. to 40. Inclusive by Way of Exposition. Besides the Remarks I made on the Several passages, as I Went on, I observd, by Way of Application, That our Lord will proceed, as Judge of all Earth, to Try, Judge and admit to heaven, upon public, Visible Evidences of Grace, or Fruits of Faith, viz: Good works—works of Charity and Mercy—Not upon Inward Experiences (Though Necessary for heaven,) but upon the Visible Fruits thereof, as the only Safe Role of public Judgement.

....

JUNE 12. 1775. This day compleats 8 Weeks Since I was here before. The Last Lecture was omitted, partly by reason of the Troublesome Times, but more officially, my Daughters *Visit* and *Marriage* happening about that Time.

This Day June 12. preachd at Mr. Deakes, only to 5 Indians, one of which was a little one—Isa: 26.9. *When thy Judgements Are in the Earth, the Inhabitants of the World will Learn Rights.* Felt in my Self exceeding barren, dead and Lifeless, And See nothing but Death among the Indians. Not the Least Encouragement from the Indians, nor in my Self, to go on with This Work; Yet did not See Clear to give it up. So appointed Another Lecture This day 4 Weeks viz: July 10th one o'Clock. Went away Sunk in Spirit—Sorrowfull—Lamenting and mourning to God my Sad and Desolate Condition! Returnd by Mr. Parks—Lodgd There. Met Cpt. *Benja.* Park here, going to Boston Camps equippd for war, if his Service is Needed.[1] Lieut. Jno. Park, Training his Company, and Recruiting, to Join the Army as soon as fall. . . .

1 Benjamin Park (1735-75) was the second child of Joseph and Abi-

gail Park. He was a captain in the Revolution and was killed at Bunker Hill, June 17, 1775 (Anonymous 1917: 15).

... JULY 10. 1775. Preachd [at] School House from Jno. 14.6. *I am the Way* etc. to 10 Indians. Had Some degree of Freedom, but low in Body and Spirit. Mr. Deake has no Schollars. Nothing Special attends This Lecture. Returned the Same day. . . .

... AUGT. 7. 1775. Mr. Deake no Schollars, but expects a few now Soon. Waited about 2 hours before one Indian Came—Then came 3 Indian Women—Too late for Lecture, being obligd to return home This day. Doctor Harry, being Very Sick, Sent word, by Mr. Deake, he desird to See me. So gave a Short Exhortation to These Three Indian Women, and then went with Mr. Deake, to Visit Doctr. Harry. Discoursd with him, Some time, as long and as much as there Seemd to be Occasion. Found him comfortable in his mind, as to his Spiritual State. He did not ask me to pray with him; So did not offer it. Took leave, not much expecting to See him again alive.

To Revd. Mr. Joseph Fish / Stonington

Charlestown the 29 of November AD 1775.

REVD. DEAR SIR,

I now acquaint you with the present uneasyness of the poor unhappy Indiens. It is so happened that the greater part of the Youths that belonged to that party of Indians that have been most favourable to the School and Lectors, have engaged in the common Cause of America: the other party which had been this seven years in Opposition have used their influence to prevent their sending the few Children that is like to remain among them, with a notion of casting off their dependence upon the Commissioners and seting up, and supporting a private Shool among themselves, that I have no expectation of having a School among them this Winter. (However, it is my thoughte that Parson Graves is at the bottom of it.) They have proceeded so far as to demand possession of the School-house, which I refused to give them. As the Commissioners was at the expence of building the House, and have a Deed of it and the Lott of Land on which it Stands, I thought it would be a point of Imprudence in me to deliver possession without advice from the Commissioners, or their Agent. Besides this, there is not a House to be had in Charleston at this season of the Year, that would accommodate my Family. 'Tis unlikely Sir, that the Commissioners can meet on this Occation, neither can they Act in Single Capacity; but their Agent may. And I dare say Your Wisdom and prudence is such, that your determination with regard to the House would be agreeable to the Commissioners when ever it comes before them; and I shall, in my difficult Situation, comply with your Advice.

I think Sir, Our Service among the Indians is to an end. Poor unhappy creatures, I should be willing to serve them, if within my power, and have prayerfully sought their best good, though the more aboundantly I have loved them, the less I be loved.

In grateful remembrance of many favours, with much respect and complements to Mrs. Fish, I am, dear Sir, Your humle. Servant.

EDWARD DEAKE

Write in great haste.

Fish papers in the Manuscript Collections of the Connecticut Historical Society.

DECR. 12. 1775. Upon a Letter of Complaint, from a Party of the Tribe of Indians, against Mr. Deake, I wrote a Line, at the Foot of Said Letter, to Honourable Esqr. Phil*lips* of Norwich, desiring Him to go with Me to Charlestown, and look into the Affair.[1] To Which Mr. Phillips replyd, by Letter, "that his coming down was Very Uncertain, but he Would Endeavour it on Monday 11th Instant. I waited at home all Monday. Mr. Phillips not Coming, I Went down This day, Tuesday the 12. Found a Number of Indians at Mr. Deakes, The Schoolhouse, And Understood there were many More at Jno. Daniels, And Some of these, at Deakes, (I was told,) went and Joind them, upon my coming. A Few of them (about a Dozen perhaps,) Which I took to be of the *Sachems* Party, So called, tarryed at the Schoolhouse All the Time, refusing to Join the Other party at Jno. Daniels.

I Waited till towards Night, expecting Sam Niles's party, So Calld, (at Jno. Daniels.) would come over and open their Case. But instead of the Body of them, only *Kit Harry* came; and told me that in as much as the Commissioners did not Come, They declind having Any thing to do With *me* in the Affair; as they had frequently complaind of Deake to Me, and I had Smoothd the Matter over etc. Which was not So; As Appears, ... Decr. 30. 1771. At Sunset a great number of *Sams* Party came in to Deakes, with whom I had Some Talk, and corrected them for their Ill Treatment of me, in withdrawing as Soon as I came, and not giving An Opportunity to discourse with them When I came down on purpose to Serve them. I told them, they were hurting themselves, not Me: and that I was very

Willing to be Excusd, from any further Trouble, if they had no further Service for Me. I told them, it was *I* that Sent for Mr. Phillips, and not *They*; So that they had no reason to decline treating with *me,* on Account of *his* not Coming.

And as to Their Objection Against Me, that I would not take any Notice of their Complaints etc. I referrd them to the Instance Above mentiond, of Decr. 30. 1771. And now Challengd them all to give one Instance of my Neglect or passing over Any Complaint, when it was properly laid before me, in a public Manner: but not *one* of them Answerd the Challenge. They were All Silent. They only Said, They Should Apply to Mr. *Phillips* themselves, and get him to Assist them. I told them it was Very Well—I was Willing they Should. And Thus Ended the Matter, for this Time.

The Indians being So Set against the Gospel Ministry; And indeed against being Under the Direction of English Ministers, That I have even concluded not to Visit them any more, Unless desird, or a Door opens to do them better Service. . . .

1 Probably William Phillips, a commissioner and treasurer of the New England Company who moved to Norwich from Boston at the start of the Revolution (Kellaway 1961: 216; Perkins 1895: 45).

. . . JANY. 22. 1776 Went to Narraganset This day, and notified Mr. Deake, (by leaving word with his Wife,) and the Indians, that I woud attend their business tomorrow 23d Jany. Being before advisd by Esqr. Phillips, I met a large Number of the Indians This day, who gave in a paper, Containing Sundry written Complaints Against their Schoolmaster, Mr. Deake: which were all heard and duely Considerd. Mr. Deake, in Reply Exculpated him Self in every Article, Save *one.* So that I could not See that he was Guilty of any Material Fault. Indeed Some of Articles of Charge, containd things that were *Unhappy,* rather than *Criminal.* It might have been more prudent to have omitted them, Considering the Jealousy and party Spirit of the Indians. But there did not appear to be Any Ill intended, nor really *done* to any of the Indians. Mr. Deakes Turning the Woman out of the house, which he had hired, in the manner he did, was wrong. Mr. Deake freely Confessd his Error (as he had done from the beginning,) And made Christian Satisfaction. But neither the woman offended, nor the rest of the Indians, would forgive him; because, They Said, he did not Confess *with a broken heart.* I told them that the Frame of the heart, was a Secret to them, and belongd to the great Judge to determine. His Visible behaviour, in Confessing, was decent and Serious: And they were bound by the Law of Christ, to Accept of it, as gospel Satisfaction, and Forgive and restore him to their Charity; Turning of them to those words of our Lord, *If thy Brother Trespass Against Thee 7 Times in a day, and Turn again and Say I repent, Thou Shalt forgive him.* But twas All to no Purpose. They woud not hearken to Me, nor to the Word of the Lord.

The Greater part of the Indians Appearing to be Settled in their Disaffection towards Mr. Deake and Determind to have him out; and So his usefullness at an End with them, He Askd a Dismission from the School *There*; Which, As *Agent* for the Commissioners I gave him, . . . only Reserving to Mr. Deake the Use of the room, in the Schoolhouse, Which he now Occupies, till Some time in the Spring coming, not fixing the Month, nor Week nor day. James Niles Junr., after the Affair was Settled and over, Askd Me What Month twas expected Mr. Deake would go out of the house? I told him, perhaps in *April* or *May,* I could not tell the particular time, as I knew not how Soon, or how long, before he could find a place to move his Family to.

And Seeing no prospect of my own further Serviceableness to These Indians, Either as Preacher or Inspector of their School Affairs, I took my final Leave of them, after a Narrative of my Conduct (in brief,) and of their Treatment of Me, Some good, Some very bad, from the Begining for 10 Years past—Giving them a Solemn admonition for neglecting and practically despising a preached Gospel, and Bible Truths, and warning of Satans recovering his Kingdom among them, as in the days of their heathenism. Thus Ends a Ten Years mission, promising as the rising Sun, in the Begining, but Setting, in Cloud.

JOSEPH FISH

....

To The Honourable
William Phillips Esqr. / Norwich

Stonington Jany. 24. 1776

HOND. SIR,

By reason of Sickness in my Family, I could by no means leave home, to Settle the disturbance at Narraganset, 'till this week. On Monday I went down, and gave Mr. Deake and the Indians Notice, that I would attend their affairs, next morning. Yesterday, the 23d. The Heads of the Indian Tribe, and many more, met me; and gave in their Complaints, fully, in writing. Due Attention was given and Notice taken of them All. In Reply, Mr. Deake Exculpated himself in every Article, that he pretended to justifie, So that it did not appear to Me, that he was chargeable with any *material fault* therein, Though Somethings were unhappily Situated, and not as I coud wish. As to his conduct in turning the woman out of her house, (which he had hired,) and using of her with Severity, (done in a heat of temper, which, it appeard, he had great provocation to,) Mr. *Deake* freely confessd his Fault therein, (as he had ever done from the Begining,) and made Christian Satisfaction to the Complainant; though neither *She* nor the *Indians* would openly forgive him, because, they Said, *he did not Confess with a Broken heart;* which, they were told, belongd to the Searcher of hearts, to Judge of. Since he Said (with visible tokens of Sincerity,) *I do repent,* twas the Comand of Christ that they *Should forgive him.* The greater part of the Tribe appearing to be disaffected towards him, and being Convincd that his usefullness was at an End, among these Indians, Mr. Deake, of his own Accord, Desird to be dismissd from his Care of them as Schoolmaster. This being agreable to the Opinion and Advice of your Last to me, (in which I fully concurr), as Agent for the Honourable Board, I dismissd him from the School there. And not Seeing the least probability of my Own Usefullness any longer among them, in the Gospel Ministry, or Affairs of the School, I took my final Leave of them presuming on the Honourable Commissioners Approbation. Thus ends a Ten years Mission, after hopefull beginings, in a Cloud! But the Seed of Gods word that has been Sown among them, though neglected and despisd, for the present, may Spring up and flourish in the rising Generation. With great respect, I am Sr. Yr. most Obedt. humle. Servt.

JOSEPH FISH

[*Inserted inverted in left margin*:] N.B. This Letter was alterd, Corrected and Substance of it transcribd and Sent.

Fish papers in the Manuscript Collections of the Connecticut Historical Society.

February 27, 1769 entry from the diary. *Photograph courtesy of the Connecticut Historical Society.*

The grave site of Joseph Fish in North Stonington, Connecticut.
Photograph by Riva Simmons.

Eighteenth-century woodcut of Samson Occom. *Photograph courtesy of the Connecticut Historical Society.*

The Church of CHRIST a firm and durable House.

SHOWN IN A

Number of SERMONS

ON

MATTH. XVI. 18.

UPON this rock I will build my church, and the gates of hell shall not prevail against it.

THE Substance of which

WAS DELIVERED

AT *STONINGTON*,

ANNO DOMINI, 1 7 6 5.

By Joseph Fish, *A. M.*

And PASTOR of a CHURCH there.

EZEK. 43. 10. *Thou son of man, shew the house to the house of Israel, that they may be ashamed of their iniquities, and let them measure the pattern.*

ROM. 9. 6. *For they are not all Israel which are of Israel.*

N E W - L O N D O N :

Printed and sold by TIMOTHY GREEN, 1767.

Title page of *The Church of Christ*, 1767. *Photograph courtesy of the Connecticut Historical Society.*

The Mission in Retrospect

THE MISSION
IN RETROSPECT

Scholars of religion have preferred to focus on the extent to which religious leaders have transformed the status quo, and scarcely anything is known about the many would-be prophets and reformers whose labors made no impression on those people whom they hoped to change. In many respects Joseph Fish was the obverse of earlier New England Puritan missionaries like John Eliot and Thomas Mayhew, Jr., and of the Seneca prophet Handsome Lake, and many others, who succeeded in reorienting American Indian religion and world view during the years of conquest and domination by European colonial populations. An understanding of his difficulties is as revealing as their successes in interpreting the role of religion in the broader process of social change.

At first appearance, Joseph Fish's problems with the Narragansett were predictable because he advocated a religious point of view that was sociologically inappropriate to Indian experience. He represented the established and conservative mainstream of New England Puritanism, and the Narragansett understandably preferred a separate current that appealed to a variety of marginal and oppressed people, including other Indians, blacks, and many English. The Indians had an added reason for embracing the New Light religion, for in its emphasis on trance, visions, the internal call, and the spoken over the written word, it resembled their ancestral shamanism. However, the existence of social and cultural differences between English Congregationalists and the Narragansett New Lights does not explain Fish's ineffectiveness as a missionary, for most historical examples of religious change and conversion involve the transference of a world view and set of sacred symbols from one distinct and sometimes very different social universe to another.

One possible explanation for Fish's inability to communicate persuasively with the Narragansett is that his understanding of their culture was shallow and judgmental. In his mind, the Narragansett represented an ordinary case of Separate errors, and he did not concern himself with questions regarding the ways in which Narragansett New Lights differed from their English brethren or the extent to which their religion revealed distinctly Indian themes. His lack of interest in their culture was not atypical of his time, for once the balance of power shifted in favor of the English, they generally perceived Indians less as an interesting culture and more as an example of moral depravity (Simmons 1981: 70-72). Fish was satisfied that their religion was wrong and did not concern himself with the subtleties of its content. However, the case for the necessity of cross-cultural understanding in successful missionary work is not self-evident, for, Joseph Park, who converted the body of the Narragansett in 1743, seems likewise to have been disinterested in their indigenous beliefs and, like Fish, glossed over cultural differences in judgmental terms. That Fish thought poorly of Narragansett practices clearly caused some resentment on their part, but his disapproval, in itself, cannot explain their unyielding resistance to his point of view.

Fish's personality contributed to some extent to his difficulties. Successful religious reformers are often known to possess the contagious and inspirational quality that Max Weber referred to as charisma (Weber 1947: 358-63; 1963: 46-59).[1] Separates in particular valued charismatic and

[1] According to Weber, the term "charisma" is applied to "a certain quality of an individual personality by virtue of which he is set apart from ordinary men and treated as endowed with supernatural

lively qualities in their preachers. Fish often complained of his inability to lecture with strong feeling, and the Narragansett sometimes expressed dissatisfaction with his dry and learned style. According to the testimony of members of his North Stonington congregation, his preaching was logical and clear, "unaccompanied by much outburst of impassioned appeal and exhortation, which made some think far less of Mr. Fish than they did of the fiery zeal ... of the 'new light' preachers" (Hubbell 1863: 10). Yet, the deadness and lack of zeal and power that Fish often complained of in his diaries did not characterize the beginning of his mission. Rather, his performance and confidence slipped gradually as he became aware that the Narragansett had closed their ears to his teaching.

The Narragansett themselves offered many reasons for their resistance, which included their dislike of hireling clergy, their belief that New Lights received their teachings directly from heaven whereas Fish stole the word of the prophets, and resentment of his attitude regarding Separates. These criticisms, however, do not appear in the early pages of the diary and did not prevent the Narragansetts' initial acceptance of and enthusiasm for the mission and school. In the first year or two, Fish perceived that the Indians were open to his teaching and perhaps willing to change themselves to his liking.

The cause of their disaffection appears partially buried beneath the reasons that they and Fish offered and becomes clearer when their entire political and economic fortunes are considered. When the Narragansett accepted Fish's offer to preach and to open a school, they did so with the expecta-

---

... or at least specifically exceptional powers. ... as are not accessible to the ordinary person, but are regarded as of divine origin or as exemplary, and on the basis of them the individual concerned is treated as a leader" (1947: 358-59).

tion that he and Deake would prove to be effective allies in their struggle for survival vis à vis the Sachem and the colonial government. Samuel Niles expressed some of these material expectations when he questioned the purpose of the school and preaching when all their lands were being sold, and when he confessed that he only befriended Fish because he provided them with a school. Fish disappointed them in his role as ally in two respects. First, he was not influential enough to persuade Andrew Oliver or Sir William Johnson to intervene in the Indians' behalf. Second, he did not try very hard to be their advocate beyond writing several letters which brought no tangible results. Also, Fish was friendly with Dr. Joshua Babcock, Col. Christopher Champlin, and others of the Rhode Island gentry who openly or tacitly approved of the selling of Indian Land—and he left no record that he attempted to influence these persons in the Indians' favor. As the Narragansett land case worsened in the fall of 1768, and as Fish's political limitations became apparent, many withdrew from school and lectures and became increasingly critical of his religion in the same terms that the Reverend James Davenport and others had denounced the Standing ministry some twenty-three years before. Real social grievances can be sensed directly behind their theological arguments. By accusing Fish of not getting his views from heaven, of stealing the word of the prophets, and of accepting wages, they were saying that he owed his allegiances elsewhere and could not challenge the society that was defeating them. The Narragansett perceived Fish as an enemy disguised as an angel and as trying to gain dominion over them. Niles's supporters turned against the school for similar reasons. Despite his original enthusiasm Niles became increasingly critical of education after their political defeats in 1768, by arguing that his preaching came directly from the Spirit while Fish only paraphrased the written word, and by discouraging learning. In both cases Niles would seem to have been expressing disappointment that Indian efforts at literacy had brought no victories in Rhode Island courts. In criticizing Deake for favoring English over Indian children, the Narragansett also revealed an apprehension that he, like Fish, was aligned with the majority society against them. As Weber (1958), Simmons (1979b), Wallace (1970: 263-302), Horton (1971; 1975a; 1975b), and others have demonstrated with respect to religion, and Ogbu (1978: 358-60) has argued with regard to education, motivation for change and commitment to a new set of values are linked to the perception that such changes will be beneficial—that they will lead to more satisfying social and cultural adaptations. In this case, the Narragansett rejected their missionary and teacher because, in their experience, neither offered hope for a successful resolution to their pressing worldly dilemmas, and, in fact, both appeared to represent the social order responsible for their suffering. Fish was sympathetic to their immediate and practical needs but was more concerned with their eligibility for the life hereafter.

Yet, Fish's Puritanism with its emphasis on steadiness, learning, scriptural authority, and family government was not irrelevant to survival in a threatening and uncertain world. According to Michael Walzer, "Puritanism appears to be a response to disorder and fear, a way of organizing men to overcome the acute sense of chaos" (Walzer 1964: 77). This faith had sustained a revolution in England, gave spirit to thousands of colonists who migrated to North America, and provided an orientation that proved adaptive to complex modern life. In his words, however, Fish did not know what method or argument to use to persuade the Narragansett of the value of his religious point of view. As they stiffened in their resistance and his following declined he suffered increasingly frequent thoughts of his own barrenness and the likelihood that God was indifferent to his work. In the latter years of his mission he looked hopefully for support from the Sachem's party, which never materialized and which inevitably worsened his relations with Niles and others who accused him and Deake of aggravating factional differences. Thus, despite a promising beginning, he feared that Satan had regained his kingdom among the Narragansett, dismissed the schoolteacher Deake, and resigned from his mission.[2]

The Narragansett mission was but one facet of Fish's life, and he continued to preach to his North Stonington congregation as well as to the Stonington Pequots. By 1776 he became increasingly absorbed in the events of the American Revolution and even made a visit to the American camp on Harlem Heights, New York, where he remained for several days in sight of the powerful British armies. Although the Narragansett were silent about his death at his North Stonington home in 1781, an aged Pequot woman insisted on seeing her minister once more and asked "Oh, Mr. Fish, are you going to leave me in this wicked world?" Fish replied, "Farewell, Esther, I hope we shall meet in Heaven" (Silliman 1857: 365). That hope had been the guiding motive of his pastoral life and his Indian missionary work.

[2] We have been unable to find any record of Edward Deake after this time. His name does not appear in the Charlestown or Westerly records and presumably he moved away.

REFERENCES CITED

Allen, William
 1857 The American Biographical Dictionary.... Boston: John
   P. Jewett and Henry P. B. Jewett.

Alston, R. C., ed.
 1967 A New Guide to the English Tongue [by Thomas Dilworth, 1751 edition]. Leeds: Scolar Press.

Anonymous
 1917 Some Account of the Park Family.... Westerly, R. I.:
   Westerly Historical Society.

Arnold, James N.
 1896 A Statement of the Case of the Narragansett Tribe of Indians, As Shown in the Manuscript Collection of Sir
   William Johnson. Newport, R. I.: Mercury Publishing
   Company.

Arnold, Samuel G.
 1860 History of the State of Rhode Island and Providence Plantations...I and II. New York: D. Appleton and Company.

Backus, Isaac
 1754 All True Ministers of the Gospel Are Called Into that
   Work by the Special Influences of the Holy Spirit. A Discourse Shewing the Nature and Necessity of an Internal
   Call.... Boston: Fowle. Reprinted in McLoughlin 1968:
   69-128.

 1764 A Letter to the Reverend Mr. Benjamin Lord .... Providence: William Goddard.

 1768 A Fish Caught in His Own Net .... Boston: Edes and Gill.
   Reprinted in McLoughlin 1968: 167-288.

 1773 A Discourse .... Together With an Address to Joseph
   Fish .... Boston: John Boyles.

 1871 A History of New England with Particular Reference to
   the Denomination of Christians Called Baptists. 2nd edi-
   tion with notes by David Weston II. Newton, Mass.:
   Backus Historical Society.

Bartlett, John Russell, ed.
 1861 Records of the Colony of Rhode Island and Providence
   Plantations, in New England, VI, 1757-1769. Providence:
   Knowles, Anthony and Company, State Printers.

 1862 Records of the Colony of Rhode Island and Providence
   Plantations, in New England, VII, 1770-1776. Providence:
   A Crawford Greene, State Printer.

Beatty, Charles
    1768   The Journal of a Two Months Tour.... London: William Davenhill and George Pearch.

Bercovitch, Sacvan
    1978   The American Jeremiad. Madison: University of Wisconsin Press.

Biographical Cyclopedia
    1881   The Biographical Cyclopedia of Representative Men of Rhode Island. Providence: National Biographical Publishing Company.

Blodgett, Harold
    1935   Samson Occom. Hanover: Dartmouth College Publications.

Boissevain, Ethel
    1975   The Narragansett People. Phoenix, Ariz.: Indian Tribal Series.

Bowden, Henry W.
    1981   American Indians and Christian Missions: Studies in Cultural Conflict. Chicago: University of Chicago Press.

Boyd, Julian P., et al., eds.
    1950   The Papers of Thomas Jefferson, Volume I, 1760-1776. Princeton: Princeton University Press.

Bragdon, Kathleen J.
    1979   Probate Records as a Source for Algonquian Ethnohistory. *In* Papers of the Tenth Algonquian Conference, William Cowan, ed., pp. 136-41. Ottawa: Carleton University.
    1981   "Another Tongue Brought In": An Ethnohistorical Study of Native Writings in Massachusett. Ph.D. dissertation, Department of Anthropology, Brown University.

Brasser, Ted J.
    1974   Riding on the Frontier's Crest: Mahican Indian Culture and Culture Change. Ottawa: National Museum of Man Mercury Series, Ethnology Division, Paper No. 13.

Burlingame, Edwin A., et al., eds.
    1925   The Narragansett Mortgage.... Providence: Society of Colonial Wars.

Bushman, Richard L.
    1967   From Puritan to Yankee: Character and the Social Order in Connecticut, 1690-1765. Cambridge: Harvard University Press.

Butterfield, Lyman H., et al., eds.
    1961   Diary and Autobiography of John Adams. Cambridge: Harvard University Press.

Campbell, Paul, and Glenn LaFantasie
    1978   Scattered to the Winds of Heaven—Narragansett Indians 1676-1880. Rhode Island History 37: 67-83.

Carpenter, Esther B.
  1924   South County Studies of Some Eighteenth Century Per-
          sons, Places and Conditions .... Boston: Merrymount Press.
Caulkins, Frances M.
  1895   History of New London, Connecticut .... New London:
          H. D. Utley.
Champlin Papers
  1751-   Ms. Credit records of Thomas Ninigret. Rhode Island
  1757   Historical Society Library.
  1753   Ms. The Deposition of Sarah Tom .... August 2, 1753.
          Rhode Island Historical Society Library.
Chapin, Howard M.
  1931   Sachems of the Narragansetts. Providence: Rhode Island
          Historical Society.
Cohen, Daniel A., ed.
  1977   Preface, pp. v-xxvii, to The New England Primer En-
          larged .... [1737 edition]. New York: Garland.
Cole, J. R.
  1889   History of Washington and Kent Counties, Rhode Island
          .... New York: W. W. Preston.
Committee of Investigation
  1880   State of Rhode Island and Providence Plantations. Narra-
          gansett Tribe of Indians, Report of the Committee of
          Investigation.... Providence: E. L. Freeman and Com-
          pany, Printers to the State.
Commuck, Thomas
  1845   Indian Melodies. New York: G. Lane and C. B. Tippett
          for the Methodist Episcopal Church.
  1859   Sketch of the Brothertown Indians. Collections of the
          State Historical Society of Wisconsin, IV. Lyman C. Dra-
          per, ed., pp. 291-98.
Conkey, Laura E., Ethel Boissevain, and Ives Goddard
  1978   Indians of Southern New England and Long Island: Late
          Period. In Handbook of North American Indians: North-
          east, XV. William Sturtevant, series ed., Bruce Trigger,
          vol. ed., pp. 177-89. Washington, D. C.: Smithsonian In-
          stitution.
Cowan, William
  1973   Narragansett 126 Years After. International Journal of
          American Linguistics 39: 7-13.
Daniels, Bruce C.
  1980   Economic Development in Colonial and Revolutionary
          Connecticut: An Overview. The William and Mary Quar-
          terly 3rd Series, 37: 429-50.

Day, Gordon M.
    1981   The Identity of the Saint Francis Indians. Ottawa: Na-
            tional Museum of Man Mercury Series. Canadian Eth-
            nology Service, Paper No. 71.
Decker, Robert O.
    1976   The Whaling City: A History of New London. Chester,
            Conn.: Pequot Press.
De Forest, John W.
    1853   History of the Indians of Connecticut from the Earliest
            Known Period to 1850. Hartford, Conn.: Wm. J. Ham-
            ersley.
Denison, Frederic
    1878   Westerly (Rhode Island) and Its Witnesses, for Two Hun-
            dred and Fifty Years, 1626-1876.... Providence: J. A. and
            R. A. Reid.
Dexter, Franklin B., ed.
    1901   The Literary Diary of Ezra Stiles ... I, January 1, 1769-
            March 13, 1776. New York: Charles Scribner's Sons.
    1916   Extracts from the Itineraries and Other Miscellanies of
            Ezra Stiles ... 1755-1794 .... New Haven: Yale University
            Press.
Fish, Joseph
    1739-   Ms. 450, Diary of Joseph Fish. Yale University Library.
    1770
    1743   Ms. Joseph Fish to Joseph Park, December 9, 1743. Yale
            University Library.
    1760   Christ Jesus the Physician .... Preach'd Before the Gen-
            eral Assembly ... of Connecticut, at Hartford, on ...
            May 8, 1760 .... New London: Timothy Green.
    1762   Ms. Joseph Fish to Andrew Oliver, November 15, 1762.
            Manuscript Collections of the Connecticut Historical So-
            ciety.
    1767   The Church of Christ a Firm and Durable House. Shown
            in a Number of Sermons .... New London: Timothy
            Green.
    1771   The Examiner Examined. Remarks on a Piece Wrote by
            Mr. Isaac Backus .... New London: Timothy Green.
Flick, Alexander C., ed.
    1925   The Papers of Sir William Johnson ... Volume IV. Al-
            bany: University of the State of New York.
    1927   The Papers of Sir William Johnson ... Volume V. Al-
            bany: University of the State of New York.
    1928   The Papers of Sir William Johnson ... Volume VI. Al-
            bany: University of the State of New York.

Forbes, Harriette M.
  1923   New England Diaries 1602-1800: A Descriptive Cata-
          logue of Diaries, Orderly Books and Sea Journals. Tops-
          field, Mass.: Perkins Press.

Gatschet, Albert S.
  1973   Narragansett Vocabulary Collected in 1879. International
          Journal of American Linguistics 39:14.

Gaustad, Edwin S.
  1957   The Great Awakening in New England. New York: Harper
          and Row.

Gilman, E. W.
  1869   Ancient Confessions of Faith and Family Covenants. The
          Congregational Quarterly XI, new series I: 516-27. Bos-
          ton: Congregational Rooms.

Goen, C. C.
  1962   Revivalism and Separatism in New England, 1740-1800:
          Strict Congregationalists and Separate Baptists in the
          Great Awakening. New Haven: Yale University Press.

Goodwin, Daniel, ed.
  1907   A History of the Episcopal Church in Narragansett . . .
          By Wilkins Updike . . . II. Boston: Merrymount Press.

Guildhall Library
  1751-   Ms. 7952, Records of the New England Company. Loose
  1753   court minutes, 1655-1816.

Hamilton, Milton W., and Albert B. Corey, eds.
  1953   The Papers of Sir William Johnson . . . Volume XI: Al-
          bany: University of the State of New York.
  1957   The Papers of Sir William Johnson . . . Volume XII. Al-
          bany: University of the State of New York.
  1962   The Papers of Sir William Johnson . . . Volume XIII. Al-
          bany: University of the State of New York.

Handlin, Oscar, et al., eds.
  1954   Harvard Guide to American History. Cambridge: Har-
          vard University Press.

Haynes, Williams
  1949   1649-1949 Stonington Chronology: Being a Year-by-Year
          Record of the American Way of Life in a Connecticut
          Town. Stonington, Conn.: Pequot Press.

Horton, Robin
  1971   African Conversion, Africa 41: 85-108.
  1975a   On the Rationality of Conversion I. Africa 45: 219-35.
  1975b   On the Rationality of Conversion II. Africa 45: 373-99.

Hubbell, Stephen
  1863   A Discourse Commemorative of the Rev. Joseph Fish
          . . . . Norwich, Conn.: Bulletin Job Office.

Hutchins, Francis G.
    1979   Mashpee: The Story of Cape Cod's Indian Town. West Franklin, N. H.: Amarta Press.

Jordan, John E.
    1962   De Quincy to Wordsworth: A Biography of a Relationship. Berkeley: University of California Press.

Kellaway, William
    1961   The New England Company 1649-1776: Missionary Society to the American Indians. London: Longmans, Green.

Kimball, Gertrude S., ed.
    1903   The Correspondence of the Colonial Governors of Rhode Island 1723-1775 ... II. Boston: Houghton, Mifflin.

Lathem, Edward C.
    1971   A Guide to the Microfilm Edition of the Papers of Eleazar Wheelock, Together with the Early Archives of Dartmouth College and Moor's Indian Charity School ... Through the Year 1779. Hanover: Dartmouth College Library.

Lauber, Almon W.
    1913   Indian Slavery in Colonial Times within the Present Limits of the United States. Columbia University Studies in History, Economics, and Public Law 54(3). New York.

Leach, Douglas E.
    1958   Flintlock and Tomahawk: New England in King Philip's War. New York: Macmillan (Reprinted: W. W. Norton, New York, 1966).

Levitas, Gloria
    1980   No Boundary Is a Boundary: Conflict and Change in a New England Indian Community. Ph.D. Dissertation, Department of Anthopology, Rutgers University. Ann Arbor: University Microfilms International.

Lewis, I. M.
    1971   Ecstatic Religion: An Anthropological Study of Spirit Possession and Shamanism. Baltimore: Penguin Books.

Lockridge, Kenneth A.
    1973   Social Change and the Meaning of the American Revolution. Journal of Social History 6: 403-39.

Love, W. De Loss
    1899   Samson Occom and the Christian Indians of New England. Boston: Pilgrim Press.

McCallum, James D., ed.
    1932   The Letters of Eleazar Wheelock's Indians. Hanover: Dartmouth College Publications.

McClure, David, and Elijah Parish

1811   Memoirs of the Rev. Eleazar Wheelock .... Newbury-
          port. Mass.: Edward Little.

McLoughlin, William G.
1967   Isaac Backus and the American Pietistic Tradition. Bos-
          ton: Little, Brown.
1968   Isaac Backus on Church, State, and Calvinism: Pamph-
          lets, 1754-1789. Cambridge: Harvard University Press.
1978   Revivals, Awakenings, and Reform: An Essay on Religion
          and Social Change in America, 1607-1977. Chicago: Uni-
          versity of Chicago Press.
1979   The Diary of Isaac Backus, I: 1741-1764, and II: 1765-
          1785. Providence: Brown University Press.

Matthews, William
1974   American Diaries in Manuscript, 1580-1954: A Descrip-
          tive Bibliography. Athens: University of Georgia Press.

Morgan, Lewis H.
1870   Systems of Consanguinity and Affinity of the Human
          Family. Washington, D. C.: Smithsonian Contributions to
          Knowledge No. 218.

Morris, Myron N.
1857   Joseph Fish. In Annals of the American Pulpit . . . I.
          William B. Sprague, ed., pp. 359-63. New York: Robert
          Carter and Brothers.

Munro-Fraser, J. P.
1880   History of Marin County, California .... San Francisco:
          Alley, Bowen.

Narragansett Indians
1768   Ms. Copy of deed of Thomas Ninigret to Indian Tribe
          with plat. Rhode Island State Archives, Narragansett Doc-
          ument 17.
1770   Ms. Record of meeting of Indian Tribe, December 1769.
          Rhode Island State Archives, Narragansett Document 21.

Nash, Gary B.
1979   The Urban Crucible: Social Change, Political Conscious-
          ness, and the Origins of the American Revolution. Cam-
          bridge: Harvard University Press.

National Cyclopaedia
1929   The National Cyclopaedia of American Biography . . .
          VI. New York: James T. White.

Ninegrett, Thomas
1765   Ms. Letter to the Commissioners of the New England
          Company, April 26, 1765. Manuscript Collections of the
          Massachusetts Historical Society.

Norton, Mary B.

1976   "My Resting Reaping Times": Sarah Osborn's Defense of Her "Unfeminine" Activities, 1767. Signs 2: 515-29.

O'Callaghan, Edmund B., ed.
1851   Documentary History of the State of New York, IV. Albany: Weed and Parsons.

Ogbu, John U.
1978   Minority Education and Caste: The American System in Cross-Cultural Perspective. New York: Academic Press.

Parke, Benjamin
1872   Extracts from the Presbyterian Church Records of Westerly, R. I. New England Historical and Genealogical Register XXVI (3): 323-27.

Parsons, Usher
1861   Indian Names of Places in Rhode Island. Providence: Knowles, Anthony.

Perkins, Mary E.
1895   Old Housees of the Antient Town of Norwich 1660-1800. Norwich, Conn.: n.p.

Phillips, Dorothy W.
1967   The Portrait of Simon Pease by Robert Feke. The Corcoran Gallery of Art Bulletin 16 (3): 5-9.

Prince, Thomas
1744   The Christian History, Containing Accounts of the Revival and Propagation of Religion in Great-Britain and America for the Year 1743. Boston: S. Kneeland and T. Green.
1745   The Christian History, Containing Accounts of the Revival and Propagation of Religion in Great-Britain and America for the year 1744. Boston: S. Kneeland and T. Green.

Rhode Island General Assembly
1774   June proceedings, Account of the Number of Inhabitants in the Colony.

Richardson, Leon B.
1933   An Indian Preacher in England .... Hanover: Dartmouth College Publications.

Ronda, James P.
1981   Generations of Faith: The Christian Indians of Martha's Vineyard. The William and Mary Quarterly 3rd Series, 38: 369-94.

Ronda, James P., and James Axtell
1978   Indian Missions: A Critical Bibliography. Bloomington: Indiana University Press, for the Newberry Library Center for the History of the American Indian Bibliographical Series, Francis Jennings, gen. ed.

Sainsbury, John A.
  1975   Indian Labor in Early Rhode Island. New England Quarterly 48: 378-93.
Salisbury, Neal
  1982   The Indians of New England: A Critical Bibliography. Bloomington: Indiana University Press, for the Newberry Library Center for the History of the American Indian Bibliographical Series, Francis Jennings, gen. ed.
Shipton, Clifford K.
  1945   Sibley's Harvard Graduates Volume VII, 1722-25 .... Boston: Massachusetts Historical Society.
  1951   Sibley's Harvard Graduates Volume VIII, 1726-30 .... Boston: Massachusetts Historical Society.
  1963   New England Life in the 18th Century: Representative Biographies from *Sibley's Harvard Graduates*. Cambridge: Harvard University Press.
Silliman, Benjamin
  1857   From Benjamin Silliman, L.L.D. *In* Annals of the American Pulpit ... I. William B. Sprague, ed., pp. 363-66. New York: Robert Carter and Brothers.
Simmons, William S.
  1976   Southern New England Shamanism: An Ethnographic Reconstruction. *In* Papers of the Seventh Algonquian Conference, 1975. William Cowan, ed., pp. 217-56. Ottawa: Carleton University.
  1978   Narragansett. *In* Handbook of North American Indians: Northeast, XV. William Sturtevant, series ed., Bruce Trigger, vol. ed., pp. 190-97. Washington: Smithsonian Institution.
  1979a   The Great Awakening and Indian Conversion in Southern New England. *In* Papers of the Tenth Algonquian Conference. William Cowan, ed., pp. 25-36. Ottawa: Carleton University.
  1979b   Conversion from Indian to Puritan. New England Quarterly 52: 197-218.
  1981   Cultural Bias in the New England Puritans' Perception of Indians. The William and Mary Quarterly 3rd series, 38: 56-72.
  1982   Red Yankees: Narragansett Conversion in the Great Awakening. American Ethnologist (in press).
Sprague, William B., ed.
  1857   Annals of the American Pulpit ... I. New York: Robert Carter and Brothers.
  1858   Annals of the American Pulpit ... III. New York: Robert Carter and Brothers.

Stiles, Ezra
    1872   Letter to Thomas Hutchinson, January 8, 1765. New England Historical and Genealogical Register 26(2): 162-63.

Stone, William L.
    1865   The Life and Times of Sir William Johnson, Bart. II. Albany: J. Munsell.

Sturtevant, William C.
    1975   Two 1761 Wigwams at Niantic, Connecticut. American Antiquity 40: 437-44.

Tracy, Joseph
    1842   The Great Awakening: A History of the Revival of Religion in the Time of Edwards and Whitefield. Boston: Tappan and Dennet; New York: Josiah Adams.

Trumbull, Benjamin
    1818   A Complete History of Connecticut . . . II. New Haven: Maltby, Goldsmith and Company and Samuel Wadsworth.

Tucker, William F.
    1877   Historical Sketch of the Town of Charlestown, in Rhode Island, from 1636 to 1876. Westerly, R. I.: G. B. and J. H. Utter.

Walker, George L.
    1897   Some Aspects of the Religious Life of New England with Special Reference to Congregationalists . . . . New York: Silver, Burdett.

Wallace, Anthony F. C.
    1970   The Death and Rebirth of the Seneca. New York: Alfred A. Knopf.

Walzer, Michael
    1964   Puritanism as a Revolutionary Ideology. History and Theory 3: 59-90.

Wanton, Joseph
    1769   Ms. Statement regarding the Narragansett petition against choosing a successor to Thomas Ninigret, December 20, 1769. Ms. Amer. 1769 D 2, in The John Carter Brown Library, Providence, R. I.

Weber, Max
    1947   Max Weber: The Theory of Social and Economic Organization. A. M. Henderson and Talcott Parsons, transl. New York: Free Press of Glencoe.
    1958   The Protestant Ethic and the Spirit of Capitalism. Talcott Parsons, transl. New York: Charles Scribner's Sons.
    1963   The Sociology of Religion. Ephraim Fischoff, transl. Boston: Beacon Press.

Weeden, William B.

1910   Early Rhode Island: A Social History of the People, New York: Grafton Press.

Weis, Frederick L.
1936   The Colonial Clergy and the Colonial Churches of New England. Lancaster: Society of the Descendants of the Colonial Clergy.

Wheeler, Grace D.
1903   The Homes of Our Ancestors in Stonington, Connecticut. Salem, Mass.: Newcomb and Gauss.

Wheeler, Richard A.
1900   History of the Town of Stonington . . . Connecticut . . . With a Genealogical Register of Stonington Families. New London, Conn.: Press of the Day Publishing Company.

INDEX